# WAS JESUS

—— A ——

# SOCIALIST?

# WAS JESUS
—— A ——
# SOCIALIST?

Why This Question Is Being Asked *Again*,
and Why the Answer Is Almost Always Wrong

## LAWRENCE W. REED

ISI
BOOKS

Wilmington, DE

Library of Congress Control Number: 2020934411

ISBN: 978-1-61017-160-1


Published in the United States by:

ISI Books
Intercollegiate Studies Institute
3901 Centerville Road
Wilmington, Delaware 19807-1938
www.isibooks.org

Manufactured in the United States of America

# Contents

# Foreword

*by Daniel Hannan*

Jesus was not a socialist. Neither was he a liberal or a conservative, a Republican or a Democrat, a Presbyterian or an Episcopalian, a jazz aficionado or a jogger. It is always anachronistic to define historical figures with reference to trends or movements that had not yet begun in their time. In the case of Jesus, it is an especially futile exercise.

You may think of Jesus as an inspiring moral teacher, or as a madman who saw visions, or as the incarnation of the Living God. But whatever view you take, one conclusion is hard to avoid. He was not primarily interested in the social or political structures around him. Although he was in our world, he wanted us to think about a different world. He often spoke in parables and metaphors because he was seeking to convey transcendent truths in earthly language.

"My kingdom is not of this world," Jesus told Pontius Pilate at his trial. "If my kingdom were of this world, then would my servants fight, that I should not be delivered to the Jews: but now is my kingdom not from hence." More than once, the Gospels record him trying to drum that point into the heads of his literal-minded disciples.

If that were all that Larry Reed's book were about, the pages that follow would be very few. "Was Jesus a socialist? No. Next question."

But, of course, the people who claim Jesus as a socialist don't actually mean that he had a fully worked-out program aimed at nationalizing the means of production, distribution, and exchange. What they mean is that his values were socialist values, that people in socialist parties today can legitimately claim to be drawing on the broad moral principles that Jesus espoused two thousand years ago. Which, in turn, raises a much more complicated and interesting question—namely, how are we to define socialism?

At this point, its defenders become oddly evasive and vague. Socialism, they tell us, is all about kindness. It's about being unselfish, about wanting to help the less fortunate, about recognizing an obligation to other people.

If that were all that socialism was, then Jesus would indeed be a socialist. So would Larry Reed, so would I, and so, reader, would you. Indeed, in my experience, a telltale characteristic of socialists is the odd belief that they have a monopoly on compassion. It takes a certain complacent laziness to dismiss your opponents as ill-intentioned rather than entertaining the idea that they might have decent reasons for disagreeing with you. Socialism, for at least some people, is a kind of eternal childishness, a determination to see the world as a Harry Potter novel, in which there are good guys and bad guys.

That outlook depends on not considering any of our actual experiences with socialism. As Larry shows in the chapters that follow, socialism gets a special pass when it comes to learning from history. Every socialist experiment ends in dictatorship and labor camps. At which point, its erstwhile cheerleaders suddenly inform us that it was never socialist in the first place, and that "real socialism" has yet to be tried.

Imagine applying that sophistry to any other ideology. Imagine, for example, arguing that it would be wrong to judge fascism by the 1930s regimes which called themselves fascist, because "real fascism" had never been tried. It would be a preposterous argument. And yet, somehow, leftists manage to get away with judging socialism as a textbook theory while judging capitalism by its necessarily imperfect real-world examples.

What is the true defining characteristic of socialism? As Larry shows, it is not compassion but coercion. Leftists are chiefly distinguished from rightists by their fondness for state action—which is another way of saying, by their readiness to deploy coercive force in what they deem to be the collective interest. The gun is usually held out of sight rather than being plonked on the table. Socialist politicians will often use phrases like "We are asking the better-off to make a fair contribution." But behind that language, if you think about it, stands the threat of prison.

Of course, there is a measure of state coercion in every organized society. There are laws that tell us which side of the road to drive on, what our children must learn, and, indeed, what taxes we must pay. The difference between right and left is that, on the right, laws are seen as a regrettable necessity rather than as a first resort.

Which brings us back to Jesus. It is hard to find any argument for coercive force in his teachings. As Larry demonstrates, Jesus was clear that he wanted people to embrace his gospel freely. That doesn't make him a libertarian. It simply reminds us that the capacity for free will is the defining feature of humanity.

Where, then, does that leave Christians today? We should start by acknowledging the border between God's realm and Caesar's. Certainly Christianity stands for moral principles. It stands, above all, for the idea that we should treat others as we should like to be treated. That idea can be interpreted in more than one way: it is no more a liberal or a conservative idea than Jesus was a socialist or a capitalist. But it should infuse our approach to worldly questions.

What it should not mean is that Christians start claiming scriptural authority for political programs. Larry and I share an affection for the philosopher and novelist C. S. Lewis, who pondered the question of how Christians should approach politics very deeply, and to whom I shall leave the final word:

> People say, "The Church ought to give us a lead." That is true if they mean it in the right way, but false if they mean it in the wrong way. By the Church they ought to mean the whole body of practicing Christians. And when they say that the Church should give us a lead, they ought to mean that some Christians—those who happen to have the right talents—should be economists and statesmen, and that all economists and statesmen should be Christians, and that their whole efforts in politics and economics should be directed to putting "Do as you would be done by" into action. If that happened, and if we others were really ready to take it, then we should find the Christian solution for our own social problems pretty quickly. But, of course, when they ask for a lead from the Church most people mean they want the clergy to put out a political program. That is silly. The clergy are those particular people within the whole Church who have been specially trained and set aside to

look after what concerns us as creatures who are going to live forever: and we are asking them to do a quite different job for which they have not been trained.

*Daniel Hannan is a writer and journalist. After seventeen years as a member of the European Parliament, campaigning for British withdrawal from the EU, he succeeded in abolishing his job in the Brexit referendum on June 23, 2016. He is the author of nine books, including the* New York Times *bestsellers* Inventing Freedom: How the English-Speaking Peoples Made the Modern World *and* The New Road to Serfdom: A Letter of Warning to America. *You can read his articles at hannan.co.uk.*

# WAS JESUS
— A —
# SOCIALIST?

# WAS JESUS A SOCIALIST?

If anyone was ever a socialist, it was Jesus.
—*Kelley Rose, Democratic Socialists of America*

It is worth remembering that Jesus was a socialist.... His
radical ideas have influenced many critics of capitalism.
—*Peter Dreier, E. P. Clapp Distinguished
Professor of Politics, Occidental College*

To the question of "What would Jesus take?"
the answer is, *everything*. Not 35 percent,
not 39.6 percent—100 percent.
—*Lawrence O'Donnell, MSNBC*

I first heard "Jesus was a socialist" some fifty years ago. I was
puzzled. Even as a teenager, I noticed that socialist countries
were the world's least free places. I understood Jesus's message
to be that the most important decision a person would make in
his or her earthly lifetime was to accept or reject him as savior.

That decision was clearly to be a personal one—an individual and voluntary choice. Jesus constantly stressed inner, spiritual renewal as far more critical to well-being than material things anyway. I wondered, "How could the same champion of free choice endorse the use of force to reduce free choice— to take stuff from some and give it to others, or to plan the economy of other people, or to seize the means of production, or even to compel people to share their possessions?" To get down into the grubby, politicized business of robbing Peter to pay Paul seemed so far beneath him, I thought.

This was also apparent to me from my earliest readings of the New Testament: Jesus never tried to buy anybody's support by promising something he would first swipe from somebody else.

Later, in graduate school, one of my professors casually pronounced Jesus a socialist. What was the basis for the professor's claim? He said that in the book of Acts, Jesus's followers sold their worldly goods and shared the proceeds communally.

Whoa! That didn't seem right to me. Is that all socialism is, just selling your stuff and sharing it? If you want, you can do that under capitalism—free and clear, no questions asked. In fact, it seemed to me that under capitalism, there's far more buying and selling and giving and sharing going on voluntarily than in socialism. Capitalists and capitalist countries are the world's biggest donors to charitable causes, and often the recipients of those donations are the impoverished victims of socialist regimes.

So at the first opportunity, I reread Acts. In chapter 2, verses 44–47, I found what the professor was referring to:

All the believers were together and had everything in common. They sold property and possessions to give to anyone who had need. Every day they continued to meet together in the temple courts. They broke bread in their homes and ate together with glad and sincere hearts, praising God and enjoying the favor of all the people.

One contradiction leapt out at me from those verses: If these early believers "had everything in common," then how could they also possess "their" homes? Were homes an exception? Or was "everything" an exaggeration, or metaphorical?

I concluded that my professor's claim was unwarranted. Even if socialism is nothing more than sharing stuff in common (which, as you'll see in chapter 1, is not the case), it was in this instance voluntary. Moreover, nothing in Acts or any other part of the New Testament suggests that this sharing was mandatory for all Christians for all time, let alone for non-Christians. Would Jesus really want our politicians to impose something like this on everybody as a way of life? That, I thought, was beyond ridiculous.

Decades later, I read this insightful comment from Art Lindsley of the Institute for Faith, Work, and Economics, in the 2014 book *For the Least of These: A Biblical Answer to Poverty*:

In this passage from Acts, there is no mention of the state at all. These early believers contributed their goods freely, without coercion, voluntarily. Elsewhere in Scripture we see that Christians are even instructed to give in just this manner, freely, for "God loves a cheerful giver" (Paul's remarks in II Corinthians 9:7). There is plenty of indication that private property rights were still in effect.

Even in the early days of the Church, the practice of selling goods and holding them in common died out as the number of believers grew. The apostle Paul, who illuminated and clarified Jesus's teachings, never commanded it. The New Testament never mentions it as a requirement, much less a government policy. So those few verses in Acts make the most sense if you understand them as *descriptive* but not *prescriptive*.

In fact, for every Christian in history who participated in an egalitarian communal arrangement, there have been thousands or even millions who didn't. Some people want to single out those few early Christians who tried it and then suggest it is somehow superior to the private-property approach that almost all other Christians (plus an awful lot of non-Christians) have embraced to one degree or another.

The Pilgrims who started the Plymouth colony in 1620 were devout Christians. And they tried something akin to what Acts describes. In the diary of the colony's first governor, William Bradford, you can read about the settlers' initial plan: They held land in common. They brought crops to a common storehouse and distributed them equally. Every person had to work for everybody else (the community), not for himself or for his family.

Did the Pilgrims live happily ever after in this collectivist utopia?

Hardly.

The "common property" helped to kill off dozens of the settlers. Governor Bradford recorded in his diary that people were happy to claim their equal share of production, but production only shrank. Slackers showed up late for work in the fields, and the hard workers resented it. It's called "human nature."

The Pilgrims were destitute. Finally, with his colony facing starvation and extinction, Bradford altered the system. He divided common property into private plots, and the new owners could produce what they wanted and then keep or trade it freely.

In Plymouth, recognizing private property and instituting some measure of free markets turned socialist failure into capitalist success. That sort of turnaround has happened so often in history that it's almost monotonous. I know of no instance in history when the reverse occurred—that is, when free markets and private property produced a disaster that socialism saved. None. For the Pilgrims as for so many others, the "people over profits" mentality produced fewer people until profit—earned as a result of one's care for his own property and his desire for improvement—saved the people.

Two hundred years after the Pilgrims, the Scottish cotton magnate Robert Owen thought he'd give socialism another spin, this time in New Harmony, Indiana. There he established a community he hoped would transcend such "evils" as individualism and self-interest. Everybody would be economically equal in an altruistic, fairy-tale society. It collapsed within two years, just like all the other "Owenite" communes it briefly inspired.

## SOCIALISM MAKES A COMEBACK

After grad school, I became an economist, a historian, and a professor myself. Through the years I continued my inquiry into the "Jesus was a socialist" claim because I kept hearing it. For example, in June 1992, London's *Daily Telegraph* reported this astonishing remark by the last leader of the Soviet Union,

Mikhail Gorbachev: "Jesus was the first socialist." Why? Because, Gorbachev said, he was "the first to seek a better life for mankind."

Surely the former Soviet leader knew that if socialism means nothing more than the pursuit of "a better life for mankind," then Jesus could hardly have been its first advocate.

Gorbachev's claim was silly. I'm opposed to socialism, and I, too, seek a better life for mankind. It's one of the many reasons I'm *not* a socialist.

In 2011, MSNBC host Lawrence O'Donnell—who calls himself a "practical European socialist"—devoted a whole segment of his prime-time show to arguing that Jesus favored the government-enforced redistribution of wealth that O'Donnell championed. Jesus was "the first recorded advocate of a progressive income tax," O'Donnell told his viewers.

We'll address O'Donnell's claims later in this book. For now, the key point is that these were exactly the kinds of specious arguments that prompted me, in 2015, finally to write about "Jesus was a socialist." The result was a small pamphlet published by the Foundation for Economic Education (FEE).

A funny thing happened around that time: socialism started making a comeback.

In May 2016, a Gallup poll revealed that 55 percent of eighteen-to-twenty-nine-year-olds had a positive image of socialism. In that year's presidential primaries, a self-described "democratic socialist," Senator Bernie Sanders of Vermont, earned more votes from voters under the age of thirty than the eventual Democratic and Republican nominees *combined*.

Few who witnessed the fall of the Berlin Wall and the collapse of the Soviet communist empire ever expected socialism to reemerge as a serious part of America's national debate, let alone a force at the ballot box. In the early 1990s, many respected commentators hailed the end of the Cold War as the triumph of democratic capitalism. Francis Fukuyama even declared it the "end of history." He wrote of "a universal evolution in the direction of capitalism."

But time has passed, and the rising generation has no memory of the Cold War or of the repeated failures of socialism. To many of these young Americans, socialism isn't a dirty word; it's an ideal.

The resurgence of socialism has only intensified. In early 2019, a Harris poll showed that half of Americans aged eighteen to thirty-nine said they would "prefer living in a socialist country." A 2019 report by the Victims of Communism Memorial Foundation revealed that more than 70 percent of millennials said they were likely to vote for a socialist.

And as socialism has come back into vogue, more and more socialists have tried to convince us that Jesus was a socialist. On Christmas Day 2016, the *Huffington Post* published Occidental College professor Peter Dreier's article "Jesus Was a Socialist." And in a 2018 story on the Democratic Socialists of America, NPR quoted one of the group's chapter leaders, Kelley Rose, saying, "If anyone was ever a socialist, it was Jesus."

Apparently this rhetoric has had an impact. According to a 2016 poll by the Barna Group, Americans think socialism aligns better with Jesus's teachings than capitalism does. And when respondents were asked which of that year's presidential candidates aligned closest to Jesus's teachings, Bernie Sanders came out on top.

So in 2019, I tackled the topic again. I recorded a five-minute video for Prager University answering the "Jesus was a socialist" claim. On YouTube, social media, and the Prager University website, the video attracted more than four million views. The response to the video convinced me that there was a hunger for this message.

## SETTING THE RECORD STRAIGHT

With this book, I aim to show you that nothing in the New Testament even hints that Jesus would support what today's socialists call for: magnifying the powers of earthly government to redistribute wealth, or impose a welfare state, or centrally plan the economy, or control the means of production. Most socialists, and increasing numbers of "progressives," support some combination of those dubious propositions. The idea that Jesus endorsed any of them is pure fantasy.

The broader point here is that it is impossible to superimpose our modern political and economic lexicon onto Jesus or, for that matter, onto anyone who walked the earth two thousand years ago. Terms such as *socialism* and *capitalism* didn't exist in the first century AD and wouldn't appear for another 1,800 years. While I don't believe it is valid to claim that Jesus was a socialist, I also don't think it is valid to argue that he was a capitalist. Neither was he a Republican or a Democrat. These are modern-day terms, and to apply any of them to Jesus is to limit him to but a fraction of who he was and what he taught.

Jesus offered no blueprint for earthly government and the laws of politicians. His concerns focused elsewhere—namely, on the sort of self-government that men and women would exercise if they followed God's law.

Those who push for massive expansions of government while claiming that Jesus would be on their side are imposing their own narrative on him. Given the ways in which socialists and progressives try to enlist Jesus in their causes, it is certainly appropriate to ask whether Jesus's teachings are sympathetic to the ethics or economics of the human concoction that we call socialism. That's the question this book attempts to answer.

My purpose here is not to proselytize for the Christian faith in general or for any denomination in particular. I freely admit that I am a Christian. Whether you are or someday might choose to be one is a matter I leave entirely to you. My aim with this book, instead, is to clear up common fallacies about Jesus that socialists and progressives use to advance their favored policies.

I hope that anyone interested in such things as truth, history, and economics—regardless of faith or lack thereof—will find this book useful.

# 1

# WHAT IS SOCIALISM?

Have you ever tried to nail Jell-O to the wall? It's easier than getting a socialist to stand pat on a definition of socialism.

Socialism becomes an endlessly moving target. So how do you approach it? Just what *is* socialism, anyway?

This is an essential question to address before you can dig into whether Jesus himself was a socialist.

## "THAT'S NOT WHAT WE MEAN!"

Karl Marx called for the abolition of private property and state ownership of the means of production. He labeled it "scientific socialism."

"But that's not what we mean!" today's socialists proclaim.

Vladimir Lenin established the Union of Soviet Socialist Republics (USSR) in 1922. He put the Soviet state in charge of every aspect of life for "the good of the people." Joseph Stalin, his mass-murdering successor, declared that Soviet socialism would perfect the "workers' paradise" that socialist intellectuals had promised.

"But that's not what we mean!" today's socialists proclaim.

Adolf Hitler and his minions "planned" the German economy and even named their political organization the National *Socialist* German Workers' Party.

"But that's not what we mean!" today's socialists proclaim.

Fifteen different republics within the Soviet empire all proclaimed themselves dedicated to socialism...until their socialist regimes collapsed between 1989 and 1991.

"But that's not what we mean!" today's socialists proclaim.

Dozens of regimes in Africa and Asia from the 1950s on committed themselves to the socialist utopia. Every single one of them elicits the same proclamation from today's socialists: "But that's not what we mean!"

Socialists all over the world rejoiced in the rise to power of socialist Hugo Chavez in Venezuela. "This *is* what we mean!" seemed to be their mantra as Chavez expropriated, nationalized, and redistributed. But within two decades, the country had become a basket case, home to a horrifying evaporation of living standards and a mass exodus of refugees. Yet you must press today's socialists to get them to say anything about Venezuela at all. When you finally get them to talk, once more you hear the familiar refrain: "But that's not what we mean!"

It's socialism until it doesn't work; then it was never socialism in the first place.

## "DEMOCRATIC" SOCIALISM?

Marxist notions linger on in dictionary definitions of socialism. Oxford Dictionaries (whose slogan is "Language Matters") define socialism as "a political and economic theory of social organization that advocates that the means of production, distribution, and exchange should be owned or regulated by the community as a whole."

Even this definition illustrates how hard it is to say what socialism is. Think about it: What does it mean to say that "the means of production, distribution, and exchange should be owned or regulated by the community as a whole"? Must a convenience store put to public vote the decisions about what to stock on its shelves or whom to hire for the night shift? Should workers be able to seize the factory where they work and then run the business by majority vote?

And what about this "regulated by the community as a whole" stuff? Have you ever known of a regulatory body composed of everybody in town, let alone all 330 million people in the country? Don't such bodies end up being nothing more than a handful of people with political power?

To confuse matters further, more and more we see a modifier attached to socialism: *democratic*.

If socialism is "democratic," does that adjective somehow bless it with legitimacy? If we vote ourselves into it, is socialism OK? We should remember that Hitler's Nazis came to power on a socialist platform via the ballot box. In the old South, the majority democratically imposed Jim Crow laws. Votes and democratic institutions have been responsible for a multitude of sins.

Regardless, "democratic socialism" has moved in from the fringes of American politics.

For example, the Democratic Socialists of America (DSA), which emerged back in 1982, saw members win election to Congress for the first time in 2018. One of the two DSA members elected that year, Alexandria Ocasio-Cortez, became a fresh face for the socialist cause. Merriam-Webster reported that Ocasio-Cortez's rise caused a 1,500 percent spike in online searches for the definition of *socialism*.

Democratic socialists love to talk about Scandinavia as their model. "That's what we mean!" they proclaim.

Take Bernie Sanders, the most prominent democratic socialist on the American scene. He has said: "When I talk about 'democratic socialist,' I'm not looking at Venezuela. I'm not looking at Cuba. I'm looking at countries like Denmark and Sweden."

But more studious observers of Scandinavia point out that these countries have no minimum-wage laws; maintain favorable business climates; offer more school choice than the United States does; operate trade-based, globalized economies; and have few if any nationalized industries.

In 2013, for example, *The Economist* described the Scandinavian countries as "stout free-traders who resist the temptation to intervene even to protect iconic companies." They rank among the easiest countries to do business in.

The Swedish scholar Dr. Nima Sanandaji, author of *Scandinavian Unexceptionalism*, tells us:

> Nordic societies did not become successful after introducing large welfare states. They were economically and socially uniquely successful already in the mid-20th century, when they combined low taxes and small welfare states with free-market systems.... Over time, the generous welfare states of Nordic nations have created massive welfare dependency, gradually eroding the strong norms of responsibility [and undermining] the region's success. This, combined with the growth-reducing effects of a large state, explains why Nordic countries have gradu-

ally over the past decades moved towards less generous welfare, market reforms, and tax cuts.

That's right: Denmark, Norway, and Sweden have purposely reduced the generous welfare states that many Americans point to as a wonderful model. The Scandinavian countries have learned that it's not socialism but capitalism that pays the bills. As former British prime minister Margaret Thatcher put it, the problem with socialists is that they "always run out of other people's money."

In 2015, the prime minister of Denmark declared: "I know that some people in the U.S. associate the Nordic model with some sort of socialism. Therefore, I would like to make one thing clear. Denmark is far from a socialist planned economy. Denmark is a market economy."

So today's socialists say, "Well, that's *not* what we mean." They advocate huge hikes in the minimum wage, sky-high taxes on business and on the rich, little if any school choice, and massive intervention in commerce—none of which looks like today's Scandinavia.

The Index of Economic Freedom, accessible online, is a good source for comparing how "capitalist" or how "socialist" each country is. The 2020 index ranked the United States #17, meaning that only sixteen countries were more economically free or "capitalist" than America. Denmark actually ranked ahead of the United States, at #8. Sweden landed just a bit behind America, at #22. Norway was #27.

The last three countries on the list were Cuba (#178), Venezuela (#179), and North Korea (#180). These are all socialist countries. They provide almost no economic freedom. Not by coincidence, they also rank among the world's very poorest countries.

The economies of Denmark, Sweden, and Norway work reasonably well not because of the socialism they have but because of the capitalism they haven't destroyed. Through tax cuts, deregulation, and privatization, they have dismantled a significant portion of the socialism they once had. Go full socialism and you get Venezuela.

## SOCIALISM EQUALS FORCE

How do we sort through all these understandings of socialism?

No matter which shade of socialism you pick—central planning, welfare statism, collectivist egalitarianism, or government ownership of the means of production—one fundamental truth applies: *it all comes down to force.*

Here's what I mean:

Under capitalism, two Girl Scouts show up at your door and ask, "Would you like to buy some cookies?" You get to say yes or no.

Under socialism, two Girl Scouts show up at your door with a SWAT team behind them. They declare, "You're going to eat these cookies and you're going to pay for them, too."

Listen to any socialist laying out his agenda and it's painfully clear that he's not offering a list of helpful tips for the suggestion box. Those "tips" must become government mandates, orders, requirements. Socialism is not voluntary. Its essence is force. It must be compulsory.

No amount of "we do it all for you" or "it's for your own good" or "we're helping people" rhetoric can erase that essential truism. What makes socialism *socialism* is the fact that you can't opt out, a point that David Boaz of the Cato Institute has made eloquently:

One difference between libertarianism [a system based on personal choice and liberty] and socialism is that a socialist society can't tolerate groups of people practicing freedom, but a libertarian society can comfortably allow people to choose voluntary socialism. If a group of people—even a very large group—wanted to purchase land and own it in common, they would be free to do so. The libertarian legal order would require only that no one be coerced into joining or giving up his property.

Some socialists say that they simply advocate "sharing," and since socialism's advocates have good intentions, it must be voluntary and beneficial, too.

Except that it never is.

Socialism of the "voluntary" variety happens only in small communities—think back to the Pilgrims, or to New Harmony. And even in those cases, socialism flops. So it's clearly not beneficial to the people who have chosen to operate under a socialist system.

To achieve socialism on any broader scale requires the use of government force. If it were voluntary, it wouldn't be socialism, and if it were widely beneficial, you wouldn't need force to create it and sustain it.

There is abundant truth in the popular internet meme that says, "Socialism: Ideas So Good They Have to Be Mandatory." Without force to shape society the way socialists want it, socialism is nothing more than a nebulous fantasy.

*National Review* writer Kevin D. Williamson made this point well in a July 2015 article when he wrote that socialism and welfare statism "are based on appeals to solidarity— solidarity that is enforced at gunpoint, if necessary." This appeal to solidarity reflects a superstitious understanding that *body politic* is not "a mere figure of speech" but rather "a substantive description of the state and the people as a unitary organism, the health of which is of such paramount importance that individual rights—property, freedom of movement, freedom of speech, freedom of association—must be curtailed or eliminated when they are perceived to be insalubrious."

This much is certain: Whether or not you want to be a part of socialism, socialists always seem to want a big part of you.

## SO WHAT IS SOCIALISM?

So that we can proceed with at least a general notion of socialism, let's work to a conclusion here.

If it concentrates power in government so that the means of production are under either the ownership or consequential direction of government officials, it's socialism.

If it concentrates power in government so that large swaths of the economy are planned not by market forces (supply and demand, entrepreneurial initiative, consumer decisions, profit and loss) but by government officials, it's socialism.

If it concentrates power in government for the purposes of leveling incomes, redistributing wealth, and creating a welfare state, it's socialism.

Concentrating power in government to achieve any of those objectives necessitates considerable use of force. Would Jesus countenance that? I hope to convince you in the remainder of this book that he didn't and wouldn't.

# 2

# THREE PARABLES

Christians and non-Christians alike acknowledge that Jesus was a great and frequent storyteller. He drew his stories from daily life so the settings were familiar to listeners. He told of everyday people (builders, sowers, servants, tenants, a burglar, a tax collector), things (a fig tree, a mustard seed), and events (a wedding). Jesus told these stories not for entertainment but for the purpose of instruction. He taught his audiences in terms they could understand, though sometimes they had to think deeply about what he said before they grasped its full meaning and implication.

Jesus's stories are known as parables. Nearly forty of them of varying lengths appear in the New Testament synoptic Gospels of Matthew, Mark, and Luke.

Economics isn't everything in life, nor was it the primary concern of Jesus, so no one should expect it to figure into more than a few of the stories Jesus told. Usually, he focused on matters of personal character, forgiveness, the divine kingdom, God's love and justice, or faith, salvation, and eschatology.

But at least three parables deal directly with topics we normally regard as economic in nature. They involve lessons about money, investment, philanthropy, and employer-employee relationships. In those cases, might a socialist find some words of sympathy from Jesus? Perhaps a hint that he frowned on free markets and private property? Maybe a nod in the direction of compulsory redistribution of wealth, progressive taxation to make incomes more equal, government ownership of the means of production, or central planning of the economy?

No. Not a word. Precisely the opposite, in fact.

## THE PARABLE OF THE WORKERS IN THE VINEYARD

Take a look at Jesus's Parable of the Workers in the Vineyard, recorded in the twentieth chapter of Matthew. Jesus told of a landowner who hired workers for his vineyard. Apparently the landowner felt some urgency to gather the grapes before they deteriorated, because he hired more and more workers throughout the day. The landowner started "early in the morning," going out to hire a first batch of workers. Jesus said:

> He agreed to pay them a denarius [the standard Roman silver coin of the time] for the day and sent them into his vineyard. About nine in the morning he went out and saw others standing in the marketplace doing nothing. He told them, "You also go and work in my vineyard, and I will pay you whatever is right." So they went.
>
> He went out again about noon and about three in the afternoon and did the same thing. About five in the afternoon he went out and found still others standing

around. He asked them, "Why have you been standing here all day long doing nothing?"

"Because no one has hired us," they answered. He said to them, "You also go and work in my vineyard."

When evening came, the owner of the vineyard said to his foreman, "Call the workers and pay them their wages, beginning with the last ones hired and going on to the first."

The workers who were hired about five in the afternoon came and each received a denarius. So when those came who were hired first, they expected to receive more. But each one of them also received a denarius. When they received it, they began to grumble against the landowner. "These who were hired last worked only one hour," they said, "and you have made them equal to us who have borne the burden of the work and the heat of the day."

But he answered one of them, "I am not being unfair to you, friend Didn't you agree to work for a denarius? Take your pay and go. I want to give the one who was hired last the same as I gave you. Don't I have the right to do what I want with my own money? Or are you envious because I am generous?"

The ingredients in this parable are: A private individual who owns land; workers whom he hires and who willingly accept his compensation offers; employment terms that involve a wide disparity of hourly wage rates; an implicit assumption that work is good and idleness is bad; claims of unfairness and inequality, though no dishonesty or breach of agreement; and an unequivocal assertion of the rights of private property and contract.

Supply and demand probably come into play here, too. As the day wore on, the landowner offered an ever higher hourly wage. He probably had to do so to attract additional workers and bring in the harvest.

None of that reads like a tract on socialism. Everything is voluntary and market-based. Jesus never mentioned government, and he never suggested greed or exploitation. The kicker is in the landowner's response to the workers who complained about their higher-earning comrades: "Don't I have the right to do what I want with my own money?"

If Jesus was a socialist, the parable probably would have ended differently. Perhaps he would have chastised the landowner for unfairness. Maybe the government would have required the landowner to raise the wages of the first group of workers. Or if Jesus's alleged socialism were of the doctrinaire Marxist variety, the landowner's property might have been nationalized and turned into a state-run commune.

Jesus's final line of the story is "So the last will be first, and the first will be last," prompting most theologians to point out that the parable is allegorical. They reason that Jesus really meant it to symbolize the Jews who were called to God's kingdom first (the "vineyard") and the Gentiles who were called later, yet all received the same ultimate reward.

But that view is not inconsistent with the more economic interpretation I've provided. We shouldn't ignore the fact that Jesus's story rests on fundamentals of private enterprise, not socialism.

If he was a socialist, or at least ambivalent on the matter, surely another of his parables would offer an opposing setting, perspective, or lesson.

Is such a parable to be found? No. None.

## THE PARABLE OF THE TALENTS

Now consider the well-known Parable of the Talents. The term *talent* here refers to a valuable coin of the time, not a skill or ability. Some biblical translations use it; others adopt "gold" in its place.

In this story, Jesus told of a man about to embark on a long journey who entrusted three servants with his money while he was gone. (Egalitarians, please note: the initial distribution was not equal). The twenty-fifth chapter of Matthew records the parable as follows:

> To one he gave five bags of gold, to another two bags, and to another one bag, each according to his ability. Then he went on his journey. The man who had received five bags of gold went at once and put his money to work and gained five bags more. So also, the one with two bags of gold gained two more. But the man who had received one bag went off, dug a hole in the ground and hid his master's money.
>
> After a long time the master of those servants returned and settled accounts with them. The man who had received five bags of gold brought the other five. "Master," he said, "you entrusted me with five bags of gold. See, I have gained five more."
>
> His master replied, "Well done, good and faithful servant! You have been faithful with a few things; I will put you in charge of many things. Come and share your master's happiness!"
>
> The man with two bags of gold also came. "Master," he said, "you entrusted me with two bags of gold; see, I have gained two more."

His master replied, "Well done, good and faithful servant! You have been faithful with a few things; I will put you in charge of many things. Come and share your master's happiness!"

Then the man who had received one bag of gold came. "Master," he said, "I knew that you are a hard man, harvesting where you have not sown and gathering where you have not scattered seed. So I was afraid and went out and hid your gold in the ground. See, here is what belongs to you."

His master replied, "You wicked, lazy servant! So you knew that I harvest where I have not sown and gather where I have not scattered seed? Well then, you should have put my money on deposit with the bankers, so that when I returned I would have received it back with interest.

"So take the bag of gold from him and give it to the one who has ten bags. For whoever has will be given more, and they will have an abundance."

Of the three men in the story, the one who did nothing with the money entrusted to him received reprimands, while the ones who invested and generated returns earned applause and rewards. In fact, the landowner took the money of the least productive and gave it to the most successful one—a kind of redistribution, but not in the direction a socialist would have expected.

As in the Parable of the Workers in the Vineyard, Jesus's words in the Parable of the Talents repeatedly upheld such critically important capitalist virtues as contract, profit, and private property.

## THE PARABLE OF THE GOOD SAMARITAN

Some years ago, I was interviewed on a television show in the Bahamas. One of the hosts expressed puzzlement when he asked me, "Mr. Reed, you say you are partial to capitalism but at the same time you are a Christian?" He stopped there. The implication? I was oblivious to some stunning contradiction.

I answered: "Yes, I am a Christian capitalist. Or call me a capitalist Christian if you want."

Then he threw at me what he thought would make me look like a fool: "What about the Parable of the Good Samaritan? Doesn't that make a case for government welfare programs and redistribution?"

It's a question I have heard all too frequently in the years since. Like my interviewer in the Bahamas, people who ask the question usually think they have landed a crushing blow. But it requires a leap of logic to conclude that the story of the Good Samaritan makes the case for the welfare state.

Let's take a look at that story, which appears in the tenth chapter of Luke. When "an expert in the law" questioned Jesus about how to earn eternal life, Jesus affirmed the imperative of loving God and one's neighbor. Hoping for an answer that might justify his own actions, the "expert" then asked, "And who is my neighbor?" Jesus responded with this story:

> A man was going down from Jerusalem to Jericho, when he was attacked by robbers. They stripped him of his clothes, beat him and went away, leaving him half dead. A priest happened to be going down the same road, and when he saw the man, he passed by on the other side.
>
> So too, a Levite, when he came to the place and saw him, passed by on the other side.

But a Samaritan, as he traveled, came where the man was; and when he saw him, he took pity on him.

He went to him and bandaged his wounds, pouring on oil and wine. Then he put the man on his own donkey, brought him to an inn and took care of him.

The next day he took out two denarii and gave them to the innkeeper. "Look after him," he said, "and when I return, I will reimburse you for any extra expense you may have."

Which of these three [Jesus asked of the expert] do you think was a neighbor to the man who fell into the hands of robbers?

The expert in the law replied, "The one who had mercy on him." Jesus told him, "Go and do likewise."

The priest in the parable passed the hapless man and didn't lift a finger. The same with the Levite, who also belonged to the religious and political establishment. Who is the hero in the story, the one who forever earned the designation of "Good"? Certainly not the two bureaucrats. Of course, it's the Samaritan, who helped the man himself, on the spot, with his own resources and of his own free will.

How could this be anything but an endorsement of private initiative and a generous, helpful spirit? The Good Samaritan did not say to the man in need, "Write a letter to the emperor" or "See your social worker" and walk on. He didn't foist an obligation onto anyone else to fix the situation. If he had done anything like that, he would probably be known today as the "Good-for-Nothing Samaritan," if he were remembered at all.

Bear in mind, too, that Jesus's audience at the time would have seen Samaritans as "the other," even as an enemy. Surely they would have been shocked to learn that a lowly Samaritan, and not the respected priest or Levite, was the hero of the story.

The Good Samaritan story makes a case for helping a needy person voluntarily out of love and compassion. The parable does not suggest that the Samaritan owed anything to the man in need or that it was the duty of a distant politician to help out with other people's money. The "goodness" here is entirely personal, charitable, and voluntary.

Now contrast that with socialism. As we saw in the previous chapter, the essence of socialism is force. Jesus frequently urged people to help one another, but he never—repeat: *never*—suggested that this be done through third-party coercion. It was to be personal and voluntary, always.

Nothing of what Jesus actually said or didn't say supports a socialist or redistributionist agenda.

Jesus was not interested in the public professions of charitableness in which the legalistic and hypocritical Pharisees were fond of engaging. He dismissed their self-serving, cheap talk. He knew it was often insincere, rarely indicative of how they conducted their personal affairs, and always a dead end.

Suppose Jesus appeared to you today and you said to him, "As proof of the charity in my heart, I assure you that I vote for politicians who take from rich Peter to pay poor Paul." I don't think he would be impressed, especially if you behave like the priest or the Levite in the Good Samaritan story.

How you vote, or what you *say* you support, doesn't make you a caring person. It's what's in your heart that matters—and what you do with your own time and resources shows where your heart really is.

Socialists aren't nearly as interested in personal reform and character development as they are in agendas for politics and government. That's where their focus is. The closest that Jesus came to that was when he talked about matters of *self*-government—things like truth telling, kindness and generosity, and being responsible, patient, humble, and faithful. Even in his Parable of the Pharisee and the Tax Collector (Luke 18:9–14), it was the tax collector's admission that he was a sinner that justified him before God, not any acts of tax collecting or redistributing.

I'm not saying that if you're a socialist, you can't be a believer in Jesus Christ. You can certainly believe in Jesus, and accept him as your personal savior, and at the same time be mistaken about a lot of earthly political and economic matters. We are, after all, human beings endowed by our Creator with a very considerable measure of free will.

But if you're looking in the parables of Jesus for evidence that he was a socialist, you're not going to find it.

# 3

# WHAT JESUS SAID (AND DIDN'T SAY) ABOUT THE RICH

Whenever I say that Jesus wasn't a socialist, I hear a familiar rejoinder: *But look at what Jesus said about rich people!*

People who raise this point usually have in mind a story related in Matthew 19 and Mark 10. A rich man asked Jesus what he must do to achieve eternal life. The man insisted that he had kept all the commandments but sensed something missing, something that his conscience told him he must still do. Jesus finally advised him (as related in Matthew): "Go, sell your possessions and give to the poor, and you will have treasure in heaven. Then come, follow me."

The man didn't like what he heard. He walked away in sadness, unwilling to part with his worldly goods.

Jesus then turned to his disciples and uttered what some interpret as a castigation of both wealth and the wealthy: "Truly I tell you, it is hard for someone who is rich to enter the kingdom of heaven. Again, I tell you, it is easier for a camel to go through the eye of a needle than for someone who is rich to enter the kingdom of God."

*That's it!* a progressive might say. *Jesus didn't like rich people. He would favor redistribution schemes so no one had too many possessions.*

MSNBC host Lawrence O'Donnell seized on this story when he said that Jesus would be in favor of taking "everything" and was "the first recorded advocate of a progressive income tax." Jesus's instructions "could not be more specific," O'Donnell concluded: "You can follow Christ's path to righteousness or you can follow the path of the damned."

But O'Donnell takes a big leap when he interprets this Gospel story as a blanket instruction.

When Jesus said, "Go, sell your possessions and give to the poor," he was addressing one particular individual. No doubt Jesus was testing the man's faith. He was extending the supreme offer to him—a chance to join the inner circle followed by eternal life thereafter. Nothing less than total commitment was required in return. Jesus knew that if his closest followers were a bunch of rich guys, other people could dismiss his message as irrelevant to the poor (who accounted for the overwhelming majority of people back then).

But did he intend this instruction to be universal? If he meant selling your possessions to be a mandate on all people for all time, wouldn't he have said so? Wouldn't he have urged the people in all his many audiences to do the same? No such instructions appear in the New Testament.

Jesus's words to and about the rich man were not a call to envy the rich, to take from the rich, or to give "free" things to the poor. No, they were a call to character.

That call was consistent with everything else Jesus said. He warned about temptations (which come in many forms, not just material wealth). Some people let their wealth rule them, rather than the other way around. In the words of the great British statesman and political philosopher Edmund Burke, "If we command our wealth, we shall be rich and free; if our wealth commands us, we are poor indeed."

In his travels, Jesus often suggested that wealth can be a temptation and a stumbling block to accepting God's word. For example, in the Parable of the Sower (Mark 4), he said, "The worries of this life, the deceitfulness of wealth and the desires for other things come in and choke the word." So his statement about the camel and the eye of a needle is best understood as a warning: Keep your priorities in order. Don't allow worldly things (which would include political power as well as material abundance) to puff you up and make you think you don't need God.

Jesus witnessed plenty of people who allowed their wealth to corrupt them or to close their eyes to larger truths. Of course, one of his original twelve disciples, Judas Iscariot, betrayed him for silver. Before that, Jesus drove the money changers from the temple in Jerusalem (Matthew 21:12–13). This incident, by the way, is one socialists and their progressive brethren are fond of citing as a condemnation of capitalist buying and selling. But note the location. The incident occurred in the holiest of places, a place of worship—God's house. Those who were using it for a different purpose—to line their pockets—were defiling it. Jesus's admonition was not to stop buying and selling for profit—which would flout many other things he said elsewhere in the Scriptures. It was to stop doing these things *in the House of God.* "Stop turning my Father's house into a market!" he said as he drove those selling doves from the temple (John 2:16). He never drove a "money changer" from a marketplace or from a bank.

It is easy to understand why Jesus would warn of material temptations. Haven't we all noticed how wealth can corrupt and sidetrack some people? It seems that every week, there's a news story about how sudden prosperity trips up a star who seemingly had everything going for him. Then he gets caught up in drugs or behavior that breaks his family apart. You can find those stories within the worlds of politics, business, entertainment, athletics, religion—well, frankly, in *any* profession.

But plenty of rich people possess the strength of character to resist the spiritual downside of material riches. I have known many such good people, and it would be grossly unfair to lump them in with the others.

The same is true of poor people, by the way. You can be poor and be of either strong or weak character. You can allow your poverty to make you bitter, resentful, neglectful, or dishonest, or you can choose to keep your integrity intact no matter the circumstances. Poverty doesn't make you automatically good, any more than wealth makes you automatically bad.

When Jesus spoke of the camel and the eye of the needle, he was *not* saying that anyone above a certain income would automatically be denied entrance into heaven. He was expressing how difficult it is for anyone to enter the kingdom of heaven if the person prioritizes material things ahead of salvation. In fact, just after mentioning the challenge the rich face, Jesus said that *no human being*—man or woman, rich or poor—can be saved entirely on his or her own. Being saved requires God's grace and a willing heart, regardless of irrelevancies such as race, origin, or wealth.

## THE PART OF THE STORY SOCIALISTS IGNORE

If one reads only Matthew's or Mark's account of the rich man, one might wrongly assume that the man was a greedy capitalist merchant. But the story is also related in Luke 18. There, the rich man is identified as a "ruler"—in other words, a public magistrate or politician of some sort.

Luke's version adds an important element that socialists often ignore. The man was a *government* official who valued material wealth above his own spiritual well-being.

Government officials at the time were notoriously corrupt. The Roman authorities were less interested in the rule of law and good government than they were in extracting revenue, one way or another. They often farmed out the collection of taxes to local officials, with built-in incentives to extort whatever they could get beyond Roman requirements and then keep the difference. We don't know whether this rich ruler was corrupt—he claimed faithfulness to the commandments. Still, his wealth may have come through the coercive power of taxation.

## ISN'T MONEY THE "ROOT OF ALL EVIL"?

Jesus never implied that accumulating wealth through peaceful commerce was wrong; he simply implored people not to allow wealth to rule them or corrupt their character. He himself benefited from the wealth and friendship of rich people. For example, Luke 8:1–3 tells us that as Jesus traveled "from one town or village to another" with his twelve disciples, several "women were helping to support them out of their own means," including Joanna, "the wife of Chuza, the manager of Herod's household." In other words, Joanna was the wife of an important official in the ruler's court. And on at least one occasion, Jesus spent the night at the home of a wealthy man (Zacchaeus in Luke 19).

But doesn't the Bible somewhere teach that money is evil, you ask?

No.

The greatest of the apostles, Paul, didn't claim that *money* was the root of all evil in the famous and often-misquoted passage from 1 Timothy. Here's what Paul actually said: "For *the love of money* is a root of all kinds of evil. Some people, eager for money, have wandered from the faith and pierced themselves with many griefs [emphasis added]."

The difference between money, on one hand, and the love of it, on the other, is colossal. Paul did not condemn money in and of itself. He understood that the love of money betrays *avarice*. The great early Christian theologian Augustine of Hippo explained why Paul recognized that money per se was not the problem:

> In the stricter meaning of the word, avarice is what is more commonly called love of money. But St. Paul in using the word intended to go from the special to the general meaning and wished avarice to be understood in the broad sense of the word.... For it was by this vice that the Devil fell, and yet he certainly did not love money but rather his own power.

Avarice of any kind, Augustine said, reflects the "perverse love of self."

Likewise, Jesus did not denounce money or even wealth in itself. In Luke 16:19–31, Jesus related the Parable of the Rich Man and Lazarus. The rich man loved and trusted his wealth, whereas the poor Lazarus loved and trusted God. When they died, the rich man went to hell while Lazarus went to heaven.

But the story is not as simple as a condemnation of wealth. Christian apologist Simon J. Kistemaker, in his book *The Parables: Understanding the Stories Jesus Told*, explains why the two men in the story ended up where they did:

> The rich man did not find himself in hell because he had lived wickedly on earth. His many relatives and friends could testify that he had been a prominent citizen and that in entertaining guests he had proved to be a most generous host. They could speak of him in glowing words of praise and commendation. However, the rich man did not deserve hellish torment for what he had done in his life on earth but for what he had failed to do. He had neglected to love God and his neighbor. He had disregarded God and his Word.

Once again, the most important thing to Jesus was not one's material wealth or lack thereof. It was where one places one's faith. And the ultimate assessment of one's faith is the province of no man or government, but of God alone.

In the Sermon on the Mount, Jesus said: "No one can serve two masters. Either you will hate the one and love the other, or you will be devoted to the one and despise the other. You cannot serve both God and money." It's never a healthy thing to "serve" money as if it were your God, which is to say that money should never compete with God as your master. But Jesus never said you couldn't *possess* wealth and *serve* God at the same time.

Nonetheless, Scripture is clear on this critical point: It's better to build up "treasures in heaven" through one's faith and character than it is to build up treasures on earth in the form of material goods. The former is eternal; the latter is fleeting. As the old saying about money goes, *you can't take it with you.*

## THE SERMON ON THE PLAIN

In chapter 6 of Luke, we find words that on the surface seem to favor the socialist perspective. The setting is "a level place" at which Jesus stopped to speak to a crowd on his way down a mountain, hence the descriptor "Sermon on the Plain." Two verses require our attention here. One is verse 20: "Blessed are you who are poor, for yours is the kingdom of God." The other is verse 24: "But woe to you who are rich, for you have already received your comfort."

It's not clear whether this chapter is Luke's account of the Sermon on the Mount, which Matthew reported more fully in his Gospel (chapters 5–7), or a different sermon. Theologians differ on that particular.

But that question does not matter for the purposes of our discussion. Here are the important questions: When Jesus spoke here of "the poor," did he refer to the "poor in spirit," as in the first Beatitude in the Sermon on the Mount, or to people who lacked material possessions? When he said, "woe to you who are rich," did he mean to cast aspersions on accumulated wealth or simply on those who put their wealth ahead of God?

To the first question, my friend Doug Stuart, CEO of the Libertarian Christian Institute, responds, "It does seem that Jesus is not simply talking about spiritual lack, but material lack, as evidenced by the obvious contrast between rich and poor." But does that mean we should oppose "all wealth anywhere and everywhere"? Stuart provides important historical context when he asks, "What does being rich indicate or symbolize in Jesus's day?" He explains:

> The New Testament was written during a time with a very different economic and sociopolitical situation from our own.... Being rich in the first century was not due to free-market engagement in highly productive enterprises, but from being part of the privileged class where labor was exploited in the ugliest of ways. Nor was being poor about having a lousy work ethic or random misfortune. Economic status was not as fluid as in free markets, people could not just "move up the ladder," and widespread economic growth did not depend on open markets as we have in capitalism. So of course, under conditions of exploitation (not voluntary exchange), we would expect nothing less than for Jesus to give warnings to that type of rich person!

In Jesus's day, too, most of the exploitation occurred at the hands of agents of the state or of cronies of the state, including many in the Jewish rabbinical hierarchy. My friend and fellow economist Jerry Bowyer emphasized this point on David Gornoski's weekly radio show, *A Neighbor's Choice*:

> The anti-wealth passages in the New Testament are always in the context of state exploitation of the poor. Jesus never, anywhere in the Gospels, confronts a single person in entrepreneurial Galilee, where he was from, about wealth. All of his confrontations about wealth occur after he goes down to Judea, which is the political capital of that ancient region.

Doug Stuart concludes that by using the phrases "blessed are you who are poor" and "woe to you who are rich," Jesus was "upending the ugly social dynamics of his day."

It's difficult to use this passage to condemn wealth today. Under free-market capitalism, we see nothing like the corruption that reigned in Jesus's time and place. Yet we see such corruption "in abundance under socialism," Stuart notes.

Imagine a person who becomes rich not through compulsion, fraud, or political connections but through wealth creation, voluntary trade, and being fair and honest to his employees and his customers. And on top of it, he never loses sight of God. He accepts Jesus as the savior he claimed to be. He gives generously and freely to assist the poor. He keeps the commandments. He seeks to live a Christian life, and when he falls short, he prays for forgiveness and attempts to mend his ways. Do you suppose Jesus would wish "woe" to him?

Of course not! That would run counter to everything else we know Jesus said about salvation and redemption.

Stuart highlights another important point: immediately after saying "blessed are you who are poor" and "woe to you who are rich," Jesus said, "Love your enemies." As Stuart explains: "What greater way to unite opposing groups together: love each other, pray for those who mistreat you, turn the other cheek. This is not a one-sided admonition, but an inclusive approach to repairing broken social structures that benefit some at the expense of the other."

Jesus condemned those who trusted in their riches instead of God, and who gained or used their riches in ways that ignored or dishonored God. That's consistent throughout the New Testament. This condemnation is *not* a general indictment against all rich people simply because they're rich.

## DEMONIZING "THE RICH"

And yet in our society today, we often do see attacks on rich people simply because they're rich.

It seems "the rich" are the number-one punching bag every political season. Candidates vying for your vote demonize the rich—and the more socialist leaning a candidate is, the more he or she does it.

It would be both unpopular and stupid for a candidate to denounce "the poor." We all know that among the poor there are both good and bad people, people who have made good choices and those who have made bad choices. We surely want to determine the difference and render our judgments and reactions accordingly. How much or how little wealth a person possesses doesn't tell us anything about the content of his or her character—just as the person's race, sex, sexual preference, or national origin doesn't. If a person is to be judged, the judgments should be based on the person's choices and behavior—that is, *by his own sins and virtues* and not by the sins and virtues of others who simply share some accidental resemblance to him.

But listen to presidential "debates" carefully and you'll see a different perspective regarding the rich. Income bigotry is on full display. You're supposed to be the victim of the rich so the politician can be your savior. The demagogue doesn't say he wants to sift the good rich from the bad rich and treat them accordingly. He wants to go after them *all*, just for their richness.

New York City mayor Bill de Blasio made income bigotry a big part of his presidential campaign. In the summer of 2019, he declared that if elected president, he would "tax the hell out of the wealthy." During one Democratic presidential debate, he even urged viewers to donate to his campaign by going to the website TaxTheHell.com.

De Blasio never gained traction with his presidential campaign. But his supporters cheered his attacks on the rich. Never mind that "taxing the hell" out of anybody might be counterproductive to philanthropy, job creation, and economic growth.

Another would-be presidential contender, former Texas congressman Beto O'Rourke, railed against the rich in virtually every speech. In September 2019, he even declared, "Rich people are going to have to allow, or be *forced* to allow, lower-income people to live near them." How's that supposed to happen? (As an aside: When he was asked at a campaign event why he gave almost nothing to charity, he said he "gave" by virtue of being in government, as if his very presence should be tax deductible.)

Just exactly who are "the rich" anyway? Political candidates don't define the term—largely because they hope that you'll think you're not part of the group they are attacking. If you have ever given much thought to who should be put on a list of "the rich," you have some idea of how slippery and arbitrary the matter is.

Consider, first of all, that in many ways the poor in America today enjoy a better standard of living than the most affluent people of Jesus's day. They benefit from many things inconceivable to people of Jesus's time—clean running water, indoor plumbing, electricity, anesthesia for surgery and dental care, and remarkable medicines and vaccines of all kinds, to say nothing of inventions like automobiles, smartphones, and televisions.

Even in our own time, it's difficult to say who is rich and who isn't. At what income level does a person go from "not rich" to "rich"? No one knows because both notions are arbitrary. A person who makes $500,000 a year but is putting three children through college and paying off a six-figure mortgage may not feel rich at all. Someone who is childless, debt-free, and making a quarter as much might be another story altogether.

Maybe we could all agree that a billionaire is a rich person. Socialists want us to despise billionaires. Senator Bernie Sanders has even said, "Billionaires should not exist." (I scoured the New Testament for something Jesus said that suggested he thought someone "should not exist" because of his or her material income. But I couldn't find a word in that regard.)

So how many billionaires are there? *Forbes* compiles the list each year. In 2019, America could claim a whopping 607 of the world's 2,187 billionaires. If you confiscated every penny of the wealth of every one of those American billionaires, you wouldn't raise enough to run the federal government for even a year at today's level of expenditures. And the next year, you'd get nothing from them because they'd be gone.

What about millionaires? America's total population exceeds 330 million; our country is home to fewer than 12 million millionaires (defined as those with a net worth—assets minus liabilities—of a million dollars or more). Most of those 12 million weren't always millionaires. They scraped together some capital, took risks others weren't willing or able to assume, hired people, created products, and then found enough willing customers to pay the bills and then some. Or perhaps they developed a talent—in music, athletics, or any number of other areas—that enabled them to attract and please large audiences.

Senator Rand Paul, in his book *The Case Against Socialism*, points out something that socialists and their progressive friends never tell you—namely, that "the rich" aren't the same from year to year: "When the left moans about the one-percenters, realize that it's not one static group of rich people but an ever-changing group of individuals rising up the income ladder. Our liberal friends would like you to believe they are sticking it to one particular group of fat cats, but it turns out that new individuals join the ranks of the successful every year."

Senator Paul asks a good question in light of the increasingly common proposals for high taxes: "Shouldn't we at least worry that if enough 'income inequality' is destroyed, perhaps the next Steve Jobs chooses to devote his time to surfing instead of entrepreneurship?"

Although socialists are obsessed with millionaires and billionaires, there just aren't enough of them to fund the programs socialists advocate—here in America or anywhere else. That's why the more socialist a country becomes, the more its middle and lower classes get soaked. Socialist policies, and even those that "democratic socialists" and other progressives favor, result in economic contraction, lower standards of living, and the magnification of political power.

## JESUS IS NEITHER "JUDGE" NOR "DIVIDER"

One last story from the Gospels offers still more evidence that it is absurd to enlist Jesus in the cause of the forced redistribution of wealth.

Luke 12 tells of the time Jesus encountered a man who wanted him to redistribute wealth in his direction. As the King James Version has it, the man implored, "Master, speak to my brother, that he divide the inheritance with me." Jesus refused, rebuking him: "Man, who made me a judge or divider over you?" Jesus continued: "Take heed, and beware of covetousness: for a man's life consisteth not in the abundance of the things which he possesseth."

And yet we are supposed to believe, with MSNBC's Lawrence O'Donnell, that Jesus really called for the government to *take* all of people's income through aggressive taxation?

Jesus warned all people not to allow ephemeral, earthly riches to take their eyes off the real prize, which is spiritual and eternal. Socialists are far more focused on those ephemeral, earthly riches than Jesus was. Worse, their focus is not on *creating* that wealth but on *taking* it and buying votes with it, even if it demoralizes the recipients whom they wish to make dependent on it.

# 4

# "THE GOSPEL OF ENVY"

Jesus's warning to "beware of covetousness" is one socialists should heed—especially if they're trying to argue that Jesus would endorse their cause.

Winston Churchill once said, "Socialism is a philosophy of failure, the creed of ignorance, and the gospel of envy."

*The gospel of envy.* Churchill was exactly right. When socialists are not naming victims, real or imagined, they are pointing the finger at villains, also real or imagined. Chief among their villains, as we have seen, are "the rich."

The philosopher Immanuel Kant defined envy as "a propensity to view the well-being of others with distress, even though it does not detract from one's own."

Kant added that envy is "a reluctance to see our own well-being overshadowed by another's because the standard we use to see how well off we are is not the intrinsic worth of our own well-being but how it compares with that of others." Envy "aims, at least in terms of one's wishes, at destroying others' good fortune."

Envy is almost as old as the world itself. It was Cain's motive for killing Abel. And politicians wield it as a powerful tool. As the Austrian-German sociologist Helmut Schoeck noted in his classic book *Envy: A Theory of Social Behavior*, "To claim 'humanitarian motives' when the motive is envy and its supposed appeasement is a favorite rhetorical device of politicians." (As we'll see in later in this book, claims of "humanitarian motives" have become central to the growing movement for "social justice.")

Envy comes in several shades. The less harmful version occurs when you count the other guy's blessings instead of your own but try to attain them for yourself peacefully—by trade or by emulating the decisions of the successful.

A more malicious type takes this form: You despise someone for who he is or what he has, and you delight in punishing him for it, in the hope that you'll benefit one way or another. Maybe you'll get some of his stuff or attain power by vilifying him.

The worst kind of envy shows up when you act to make sure *no one* can possess what the successful person has, because you find equality in misery more virtuous than inequality.

This last version manifests itself in a tactic that politicians have used for ages—evidenced at least as far back as the sad, final decades of the old Roman Republic. I know of no moment in history in which the encouragement or practice of widespread envy produced anything but a bad outcome.

If you went looking for a scriptural passage that endorses envy, you'd be signing on to a fool's errand.

For good reasons, envy counts among the Seven Deadly Sins. It builds up nothing but concentrated state power; it tears down everything from the object of the envy (such as "the rich") to the souls of the envious themselves.

The Tenth Commandment warns of envy's close relative, "coveting." Many passages from both the Old and New Testaments caution against envy, including Proverbs 14:30 ("A heart at peace gives life to the body, but envy rots the bones") and James 3:16 ("For where you have envy and selfish ambition, there you find disorder and every evil practice").

In 1 Corinthians, the apostle Paul wrote: "Love is patient, love is kind. It does not envy, it does not boast, it is not proud. It does not dishonor others, it is not self-seeking, it is not easily angered, it keeps no record of wrongs. Love does not delight in evil but rejoices with the truth."

Jesus himself said: "What comes out of a person is what defiles him. For it is from within, out of a person's heart, that evil thoughts come" (Mark 7:20–22). He then offered a dozen evil thoughts as examples, one of them being envy.

Christian doctrine also cautions against greed, which is tantamount to the worship of *things*. So does economist Thomas Sowell, who adds an interesting dimension: "I have never understood why it is 'greed' to want to keep the money you have earned but *not* greed to want to take somebody else's money." If greed is a desire for lots of something that isn't yours, then socialists are among the world's greediest people.

Using the power of government to confiscate someone's property because that person has more than you doesn't exactly convey a pure motive.

## GRATITUDE

Although you won't find any endorsements of envy in the Bible, you will find many expressions of an emotion at the opposite end of the spectrum: *gratitude*. For example, in

Matthew 15:36, Jesus "took the seven loaves and the fish, and when he had given thanks, he broke them and gave them to the disciples, and they in turn to the people." In John 11:41–42, Jesus looked up and said: "Father, I thank you that you have heard me. I knew that you always hear me, but I said this for the benefit of the people standing here, that they may believe that you sent me."

In the 2007 book *Thanks! How the New Science of Gratitude Can Make You Happier*, Dr. Robert A. Emmons reveals groundbreaking research into gratitude, a previously under-examined emotion. As Emmons defines the term, gratitude acknowledges that (1) good things have come your way and (2) those good things arose at least in part through something or someone *other than yourself.*

Dr. Emmons documents the power of gratitude. Years of research by his team show that "grateful people experience higher levels of positive emotions such as joy, enthusiasm, love, happiness, and optimism, and that the practice of gratitude as a discipline protects a person from the destructive impulses of envy, resentment, greed, and bitterness."

That reminded me of the "fruits of the Spirit" that the apostle Paul listed in Galatians 5:22—love, joy, peace, forbearance, kindness, goodness, faithfulness, gentleness, and self-control.

But gratitude is by no means the exclusive province of Christians. Consider the case of Anne Frank.

Anne was thirteen years old when her family went into hiding from the Nazis. The Franks, who were Jewish, had fled Germany when the Nazis came to power in 1933. Anne was only four then. The Franks sought refuge in Amsterdam but were trapped there when Hitler occupied the Netherlands in May 1940. Two years later, with the persecution of Jews escalating, the entire family hid in a secret annex behind a book-case, a tiny space in which they lived for two years.

Imagine it. Living each day crammed in this secret space, knowing that without notice you might be found and hauled off to near-certain death at a concentration camp.

And indeed, the Nazis discovered Anne and her family in August 1944. They were sent to the Bergen-Belsen camp, where Anne died in March 1945, just three months before her sixteenth birthday and only a month before the Allies liberated the camps.

And yet the diary that Anne kept during this time—which posthumously became one of the world's best-known books, *The Diary of a Young Girl*—displays a remarkable amount of optimism amid so much horror. How was it possible for a youngster to see so much light in a dark world?

"How wonderful it is," Anne wrote in the Amsterdam secret annex, "that no one has to wait, but can start right now to gradually change the world."

This entry from April 5, 1944, will touch almost anybody's heart: "I don't want to have lived in vain like most people. I want to be useful or bring enjoyment to all people, even those I've never met."

Her diary is full of such uplifting sentiments. One would expect to find endless tales about the privations and claustrophobia of confinement, fearing discovery at any moment. Not from this girl. Yes, there are dark moments and candid admissions of disappointment and doubt. But just when you think she's down and out, she offers observations like "In spite of everything, I still believe that people are really good at heart."

Anne Frank's diary conveys an attitude of optimism, hope, service to others, and, perhaps most important of all, *gratitude* for the good she saw in a war-torn world.

## "GRATITUDE IS HAPPINESS DOUBLED BY WONDER"

A proper understanding of gratitude is essential to our discussion of socialism and redistributionism. Have you ever noticed the approach of most socialists and progressives? They tend to operate from a perspective of condemnation, even anger—anger at "the rich," "the system," "inequality," you name it.

In a speech in 2013, the highly regarded political thinker Yuval Levin astutely observed that conservatives and libertarians "tend to begin from gratitude for what is good and what works in our society and then strive to build on it." By contrast, he said, progressives "tend to begin from outrage at what is bad and broken and seek to uproot it."

Thus we hear attacks on "the rich" rather than thanks expressed to the wealth creators. We hear "you didn't build that!" instead of gratitude for the jobs provided as well as the goods and services brought to citizens.

Author David Harsanyi captured the socialist mindset in an article for *Reason* in July 2018:

> Socialists like to blame every inequity, the actions of every greedy criminal, every downturn and every social ill on the injustice of capitalism. But none of them admit that capitalism has been the most effective way to eliminate poverty in history. Today, in former socialist states like India, there have been big reductions in poverty thanks to increased capitalism. In China, where communism sadly still deprives more than a billion people of their basic rights, hundreds of millions benefit from a system that is slowly shedding socialism. Since the fall of the Soviet Union, the extreme poverty rate in the

world has been cut in half. And it didn't happen because Southeast Asians were raising the minimum wage.

As Dr. Emmons has documented, a grateful attitude enriches life. It elevates, energizes, inspires, and transforms. Research shows that gratitude is indispensable to happiness (the more of it you can muster, the happier you'll be) and that happiness adds as many as *nine years* to life expectancy.

Gratitude is much more than a warm sentiment. And it does not come automatically, unthinkingly. Some people feel and express it all too rarely. As grateful a person as you may think you are, chances are you can develop an even more grateful attitude. Doing so carries ample rewards that more than compensate for the task's moral and intellectual challenges.

English writer, poet, and philosopher G. K. Chesterton once said, "I would maintain that thanks are the highest form of thought; and that gratitude is happiness doubled by wonder."

Think about that, especially Chesterton's use of the word *wonder*. It means "awe" or "amazement." The least thankful people tend to be those who are rarely awed or amazed, in spite of the extraordinary beauty, gifts, and achievements that surround us.

## AWE IS AWESOME

A shortage of wonder is a source of considerable error and unhappiness in the world. What should astonish us all, some take for granted or even expect as an entitlement.

We enjoy an endless stream of labor-saving, life-enriching inventions. We're surrounded by abundance in markets for everything from food to shoes to books. In hours we travel distances that required weeks or months of discomfort for our recent ancestors.

In America, life expectancy at age sixty is up by about eight years since 1900, while life expectancy at birth has increased by an incredible thirty years. The top three causes of death in 1900 were pneumonia, tuberculosis, and gastrointestinal infections. Today, we live healthier lives and we live long enough to die mainly from illnesses (such as heart disease and cancer) that are degenerative, aging-related problems.

Technology, communications, and transportation have all progressed so much over the past century that hardly a library in the world could document the stunning accomplishments. I still marvel every day that I can call a friend in China from my car or find the nearest coffee shop by using an app on my phone. I'm in awe every time I take a coast-to-coast flight, while the guy next to me complains that the flight attendant doesn't have any ketchup for his omelet.

None of these things that should inspire wonderment were inevitable, automatic, or guaranteed. Almost all of them come our way by incentive, self-interest, and the profit motive, from people who gift their creativity to us not because they are ordered to but because of the reward and sense of accomplishment they derive when they do. It may come as a surprise to socialists, but the vast majority of what's good in the world comes not from the state but from private, voluntary, peaceful, and mutually beneficial interactions that people engage in every single day.

Some see this and are amazed and grateful. Others see it and are jaded and unappreciative.

Which are you?

Anne Frank's message reminds us that, no matter the circumstances, we can brighten our lives and those of others around us. If someone as deprived, isolated, and threatened as Anne Frank can exude gratitude, what excuse do we have today for not being thankful? With the wealth and opportunities in our midst, in spite of all the challenges we know we also have, we have every reason to be extraordinarily grateful—not just for our material abundance but also for the fellow citizens who made it possible. That includes laborers, farmers, investors, bankers, service workers, moms and dads, teachers, people of all walks of life.

And yes, that includes "the rich."

## HEROES I'M GRATEFUL FOR

It's hard to cultivate a grateful spirit if you're always counting the other guy's blessings instead of your own. So in the spirit of gratitude, let's consider the kinds of heroes whom socialists would lump into their favorite group to attack, "the rich."

One is Richard K. Ransom, founder of Hickory Farms. I learned about Ransom only after he died in 2016 at the age of ninety-six.

The *New York Times* obituary explained that not long after returning from fighting for his country in the Pacific theater of World War II, a young Ransom grew "tired of driving a vegetable truck around rural Ohio for his parents' wholesale produce business. So he started selling hand-cut cheeses at flower shows and boat shows. Soon he added summer sausage, then expanded to county fairs around the Midwest. By the time he sold it in 1980, Hickory Farms was a $164-million-dollar-a-year specialty food business."

One of the pioneering features of his stores was the free sample. Lots of them. Free cheese. Free sausage. Free crackers.

Imagine that: giving free food to people whether they actually became customers or not. But of course, an awful lot of them did become customers, because they liked what he offered.

Ransom appears to have lived a good and full life: active in community affairs and philanthropy; married to the same woman for sixty-three years; father of four, grandfather of nine, great-grandfather of twelve; a leader on the boards of local banks, a private school, and the Toledo Zoo; and a fundraiser for children's charities ever since he witnessed the suffering of children on the island of Okinawa.

A longtime associate summed up Ransom for the *Toledo Blade*: "He had really good basic values—honesty, integrity. He could relate to people and could make great friends that would last."

Here was a man who built a fine enterprise from scratch. It brought employment and goods and services to a great many people. It was successful enough that it surely put him in what some would disdain as the "one percent" of income earners. But his personal wealth represented an insignificant fraction of what he created and a small price for the rest of us to pay for the risks he took. He and his company paid millions in taxes over the years, much of which politicians and bureaucracies squandered. Then he founded a wonderful charity and became a generous donor to others.

By what twisted principle of justice do we sneer at successful people like Ransom? Did the wealth he created make someone else poorer? He gave the world far more than he took from it.

I didn't know Ransom personally, but I have known other heroes. One was the late William Law, a longtime member of the board of trustees of an organization I ran, the Foundation for Economic Education (FEE). Bill ran a Wisconsin company, Cudahy Tanning, for years. I remember him not only as a competent business manager but also as a kind and generous man. Principled, too. At a time when others in his industry were clamoring for government to keep out foreign competition, Bill stood firm and said he would never ask government to use its police power to go after his competitors. That was dirty business, he felt.

Another one is Ethelmae Humphreys, who has become a close friend and whom I admire tremendously. Back in the 1950s, she began running TAMKO Building Products in Joplin, Missouri. She was probably the only female executive in the roofing industry—and she was only in her twenties! "The thought that I was in over my head must have entered my mind at some point," Ethelmae has said, "but the situation didn't frustrate me because I'd always been told and believed that I really could do anything that I set my mind to—so I went about doing it." Leading the way at TAMKO, including serving as board chair for decades, she transformed the company from a small, local shingle maker into a thriving national firm. Ethelmae's principles are the same as the company's: "work hard, do your best, be fair and honest, and hire people you can trust to do the same." I am one of legions of people who respect her character, acumen, and achievements.

Ned Gallun was another hero of the business world. In 1958, Ned bought a company in his town of Mayville, Wisconsin. He changed the company's name to Metalcraft of Mayville and helped it become an industry leader. To this day, Metalcraft of Mayville produces the best commercial lawn mowers and lawn-maintenance equipment money can buy. In good times and bad, Ned kept the company going and growing. It now provides direct employment for nearly a thousand people. You could never meet a nicer guy.

I'm grateful for the Richard Ransoms, Bill Laws, Ethel-mae Humphreyses, and Ned Galluns of the world. They did so much to lift people up, and no one ordered them to do it. They don't deserve to be lumped in with the few who get their wealth dishonestly or through friends in government who give them special favors.

In any other walk of life but politics, demonizing an entire class of people with sweeping verdicts would be dismissed as bigotry. We would see through the demagogue's flimsy logic. We would condemn the demagogue for his carelessness, cruelty, and ignorance.

But in America today, the demonizing of the rich—the "gospel of envy"—turns out huge, cheering throngs.

According to many politicians, we're not supposed to be grateful for the good things the Richard Ransoms did; rather, we should be angry that they didn't give us even more. That sounds like envy to me.

# 5

# THE REAL MEANING OF "RENDER UNTO CAESAR"

**G**overnment, whether big or small, is the only entity in society that possesses a legal monopoly over the use of force. That's not a hyperbolic statement. It's fact. Government is not like the Girl Scouts or the Rotary Club. It has jails and it has guns, even if you don't.

When government keeps the peace and punishes harmdoers, adjudicates disputes through a fair and honest judicial system, and treats people equally before its laws, it encourages civil society and commerce. It performs a positive good. Nations that have crafted governments limited to these basic functions allow people and markets to create, innovate, and raise standards of living. But those that license government to micromanage the lives and economy of peaceful people have a much different experience. They invariably yield corruption, violence, tyranny, and poverty.

Thomas Jefferson, in his First Inaugural Address in 1801, expressed the point eloquently:

Still one thing more, fellow citizens—a wise and frugal government, which shall restrain men from injuring one another, which shall leave them otherwise free to regulate their own pursuits of industry and improvement, and shall not take from the mouth of labor the bread it has earned. This is the sum of good government.

The more force government initiates against people, the more it subordinates the choices of the ruled to the whims of their rulers—that is, the more socialist it becomes. A reader may object to this description by insisting that to "socialize" something is to simply "share" it and "help people" in the process. But *how* are you "socializing" and "helping"? It's how you do it that defines the system. Do it through the use of force, and it's socialism. Do it through persuasion, free will, and respect for property rights, and it's something else entirely.

Remember, in a nonsocialist, market-based (or capitalist) society, you're free to share all you want. Arguably, far more sharing goes on in capitalist societies than in socialist ones, but it's not compulsory. In nonsocialist, market-based societies, you're free to help people. And arguably, far more help happens freely and voluntarily in such societies than happens in socialist societies. When a hurricane hits, private entities like Walmart, Waffle House, and the Red Cross help more people in the United States than most governments in the world would help if the hurricane struck their own people.

If you add to capitalist production the Christian ethic of service to those in need, you've got the most powerful juggernaut for "helping people" that the world has ever known.

Wait a minute! you say. Jesus endorsed government—a *big* one, in fact—in his response to a question about whether it was right to pay a tax the Roman Empire had imposed. The Pharisees tried to trick Jesus into denouncing the tax. Instead he answered (in the American Standard Version), "Render unto Caesar the things that are Caesar's, and unto God the things that are God's." This is found in Matthew 22:15–22, Mark 12:13–17, and Luke 20:19–25.

In Luke's account, we learn the sinister backdrop to the Pharisees' question. The New International Version tells it:

> The teachers of the law and the chief priests looked for a way to arrest him immediately, because they knew he had spoken…against them. But they were afraid of the people. Keeping a close watch on him, they sent spies, who pretended to be sincere. They hoped to catch Jesus in something he said, so that they might hand him over to the power and authority of the governor.

Let's examine Jesus's words closely here. Again, they were "Render unto Caesar the things that are Caesar's, and unto God the things that are God's."

Notice that everything depends on just what truly *did* belong to Caesar and what didn't. That distinction amounts to a powerful endorsement of property rights: to say certain things "are" anyone's assumes ownership. Note, too, that the reference is to a particular individual (Caesar) as opposed to some nebulous collective. Sorry, socialists, but Jesus said nothing like "It belongs to Caesar if Caesar simply says it does, no matter how much he wants, how he gets it, or how he chooses to spend it." He cleverly circumvented the Pharisees' trap. Even an anarchist, who opposes all government, could embrace what Jesus said because he spoke of the rightful ownership of property.

Jesus's "render" response merely acknowledged that governments have temporal authority on earth. As he later said to Pontius Pilate, "My kingdom is not of this world" (John 18:36). But anyone familiar with the history of that period knows that Jesus would not and could not have endorsed Caesar's policies and choices.

The Caesar of whom Jesus spoke was Tiberius Caesar, who ruled the Roman Empire from AD 14 to 37. Tiberius enslaved millions. His rule, according to the Roman historian Tacitus, was "unjust and criminal." The emperor was "infamous for his cruelty and debaucheries," a power-besotted tyrant who "plunged into every wickedness and disgrace."

Can anyone in his right mind believe that by saying "render unto Caesar," Jesus was *endorsing* Tiberius's tyranny?

## UPHOLDING WHICH LAW?

But, you ask, didn't Jesus say he came to uphold the law?

Yes, in Matthew 5:17 he declared, "Do not think that I have come to abolish the Law or the Prophets; I have not come to abolish them but to fulfill them." In Luke 24:44, he clarified this when he said, "Everything must be fulfilled that is written about me in the Law of Moses, the Prophets and the Psalms." He didn't declare, "Whatever laws the government passes, I'm all for." He was speaking specifically of the Mosaic law (primarily the Ten Commandments) and the prophecies of his own coming.

Consider the eighth of those Ten Commandments: "You shall not steal." Note the period after the word *steal*. This admonition does not read, "You shall not steal unless the other guy has more than you do," or "You shall not steal unless you're absolutely positive you can spend it better than the guy who earned it." Nor does it say, "You shall not steal, but it's OK to hire someone else, like a politician, to do it for you."

In case people were still tempted to steal, the Tenth Commandment addresses one of the principal motives for stealing (and for redistribution): "You shall not covet." In other words, if it's not yours, keep your fingers off it.

Once again, it's a leap for anyone—socialist or not—to claim that "to uphold the law" meant that Jesus offered unqualified acceptance of whatever earthly government commanded.

Romans 13, written by the apostle Paul, is often cited as Christian justification for whatever governments or politicians want to do. Paul urged submission to the "governing authorities" and warned against rebellion. He also said that anyone who owed taxes should pay those taxes. So a socialist or progressive of today would say that this blesses all sorts of things the state wants to do either *for* you or *to* you, whether it's redistribution, a welfare state, foreign adventurism, or anything else.

Here, as in all other parts of the Bible, context is important. Paul was speaking to early Christians in an environment seething with anti-Roman feeling. He undoubtedly did not want provocations against the Romans to sidetrack the growth of Christianity, since Rome would brutally repress such provocations. As Dr. Norman Horn wrote in an award-winning paper on the theology of the state in the New Testament, "Paul knew full well the power of Nero and the potential harm he could cause to Christians in Rome—he calls it 'the sword'—and he does not want believers to be persecuted for anything other than the name of Christ and what he stands for." Paul set the people's sights on what he regarded as higher things of greater immediate importance.

That perspective also explains why Paul urged Christians to pay their taxes. In Dr. Horn's words: "Refusal to pay would identify them as part of the tax rebels and political rogues of the day and would give the Romans a reason to persecute Christians in Rome and perhaps throughout the empire. Paul wanted the Roman Christians to avoid becoming public spectacles and government targets."

Dr. Horn adds, "There is no compelling reason to think that Paul was deliberately writing about any particular rulers other than those in the first century Roman Empire." It would be a major error to "abstract this verse from its cultural context and make it an absolute requirement on all cultures at all times." Dr. Horn concludes, "To do so would be to put Christians under a great bondage to bad public policy."

It strains credulity to suggest that, had Jesus been preaching just before the exodus of the Jews from Egypt, he would have declared, "Pharaoh demands that you stay, and he's the law, so unpack those bags and get back to work!"

The Bible, in fact, is full of stories about people who bravely resisted the overreach of governments. Dr. Horn notes numerous instances from both the Old and New Testaments:

> Hebrews defying Pharaoh's decrees to murder their infants (Exodus 1); Rahab lying to the King of Jericho about the Hebrew spies (Joshua 2); Ehud deceiving the king's ministers and assassinating the king (Judges 3); Daniel, Shadrach, Meshach, and Abednego refusing to comply with the king's decrees, and miraculously saved twice for doing so (Daniel 3 and 6); the Magi from the East disobeying Herod's direct orders (Matthew 2); and Peter and John choosing to obey God rather than men (Acts 5).

One of my former colleagues at the Foundation for Economic Education (FEE) made a similar point: "Mary, Jesus, and Joseph fled Bethlehem rather than submit to Herod's order to kill all infants. If Romans 13 meant that everyone must submit always, Jesus would have been murdered in the weeks after his birth."

So it's an egregious error to use Romans 13 to justify one particular view of the role of government, namely a progressive or socialist one.

Suppose the "governing authorities" run a minimal state with constitutional limitations on political power and guarantees of personal liberties and private property. Nothing in Romans 13 says those governing authorities are owed any less respect than if they were socialist, welfare-state redistributionists. Romans 13 asserts the legitimacy of government per se but does not ordain what today's progressives and socialists demand.

## JESUS AND THE TAX COLLECTORS

Socialists are fond of tax collectors and tax collecting. I've never heard of one who doesn't want to dramatically boost the government's revenues and give the IRS more staff and authority to get it. It might surprise them to know that tax collectors get uniformly bad press in the New Testament.

Jesus called a tax collector, Matthew, to be one of his twelve disciples, but Matthew had to give up tax collecting to qualify.

In Luke 3, we learn that tax collectors approached John the Baptist to be baptized. They asked John what they should do. He replied, "Don't collect any more than you are required to." He added, "Don't extort money and don't accuse people falsely—be content with your pay." Of course, threat is implicit in the business of taxation. What makes a tax a tax is that it's not optional. Don't pay it, go to jail.

Jesus praised John the Baptist in Luke 7, whereupon it's reported: "When they heard this, all the people—even the tax collectors—agreed that God's way was right, for they had been baptized by John." Yes, *even* the tax collectors!

Tax collectors in Roman-occupied Palestine were widely disliked. Mark 2 reports that "many tax collectors and sinners" had dinner with Jesus at the home of Matthew. "Why does he eat with tax collectors and sinners?" people asked. Jesus responded, "Healthy people don't need a physician, but sick ones do. I did not come to call righteous people, but sinners."

In Matthew 5, Jesus urged people to love their enemies. "If you love only those who love you," he asked, "what reward will you get? Are not even the tax collectors doing that?"

How should Christians deal with sinners within the church who would not listen to the warnings of their brothers and sisters? In Matthew 18:17, Jesus advised, "If they still refuse to listen, tell it to the church; and if they refuse to listen even to the church, treat them as you would a pagan or a tax collector."

Luke 19 tells the story of Jesus's encounter with the rich tax collector of Jericho, Zacchaeus. Jesus surprised Zacchaeus by announcing that he would stay at the tax collector's home. Moved by the mercy Jesus showed him, Zacchaeus promised to return fourfold the money he had cheated out of taxpayers.

When Jesus did pay a tax, it was with reluctance. He knew he couldn't preach from inside a prison cell. Matthew 17:24–27 illustrates this:

After Jesus and his disciples arrived in Capernaum, the collectors of the two-drachma temple tax came to Peter and asked, "Doesn't your teacher pay the temple tax?"

"Yes, he does," he replied.

When Peter came into the house, Jesus was the first to speak. "What do you think, Simon?" he asked. "From whom do the kings of the earth collect duty and taxes—from their own children or from others?"

"From others," Peter answered.

"Then the children are exempt," Jesus said to him. "But so that we may not cause offense, go to the lake and throw out your line. Take the first fish you catch; open its mouth and you will find a four-drachma coin. Take it and give it to them for my tax and yours."

Let's remember this, too: One of the charges against Jesus at his trial was that he condoned tax evasion, which hardly squares with the view that the "render unto Caesar" passage presented a blank check for whatever Caesar demanded.

To be fair, tax collectors are never popular anywhere—especially if they're involved in collecting taxes for a foreign occupier. So let's be careful not to read too much into their negative portrayal throughout the New Testament. Let's simply note that Jesus spoke favorably of them only when they backed off their tax collecting. I don't have a problem with that, but socialists and progressives might.

## GOVERNMENT POWER

Jesus knew firsthand that government power can easily be excessive and evil.

Shortly after his birth, his family was on the run from the authorities. Thirty-three years later, he was killed by a government in cahoots with corrupt religious officials. During his three-year ministry, he evaded ruling authorities frequently. He rejected Satan's offer to give him command of all the governments of the world. He disobeyed the regulations of the Jewish hierarchy, particularly those of the Pharisees and the Sadducees. In Luke 11:46, he rebuked the authorities with these words: "And you experts in the law, woe to you, because you load people down with burdens they can hardly carry, and you yourselves will not lift one finger to help them."

In Matthew 20:25–27, Jesus offered a powerful statement to his followers about leadership and power. These words remind us that men and women of God should pursue humble service, not control over others:

> You know that the rulers of the Gentiles lord it over them, and their high officials exercise authority over them. Not so with you. Instead, whoever wants to become great among you must be your servant, and whoever wants to be first must be your slave—just as the Son of Man did not come to be served, but to serve, and to give his life as a ransom for many.

No book about socialism would be complete without some attention to the intellectual godfather of its most concentrated, modern essence. That, of course, would be Karl Marx, whose 1848 book, *The Communist Manifesto*, spelled out Marx's vision of a socialist society. It was to be the last stage of historical evolution before the all-powerful socialist state would mysteriously "wither away" into a communist utopia.

No other human being ever concocted ideas that produced more mayhem than Marx, and few were as reprehensible in the way they lived their personal lives. In his book *Intellectuals*, historian Paul Johnson devotes a revealing chapter to Marx. The man that socialists find to be occasionally eccentric at worst and an insightful prophet at best was, Johnson writes, "angry and hate-filled, quarrelsome, neglectful of his family, lazy, and violent."

> He suffered from hideous carbuncles in part because he almost never bathed. Some of the most memorable phrases from his two books were lifted from others without appropriate credit. He spent almost all his time at home or in libraries, and almost none where the workers he fumed about actually worked. He mooched off of others all his life, prompting his mother to say that she wished Karl would "accumulate capital instead of just writing about it."

Marx was a racist and an anti-Semite with a vicious temper ("Jewish n****r" was one of his favorite epithets). On a good day, he enjoyed threatening those who disagreed with him by blurting, "I will annihilate you!" He was cruel to his family and anyone who crossed him.

This is the man who postured as a thinker whose ideas would save humanity.

Marx embodied a problem that the philosopher Eric Hoffer identified in the twentieth century: "Scratch an intellectual, and you find a would-be aristocrat who loathes the sight, the sound and the smell of common folk." Hoffer, the "longshoreman philosopher," proved the exception to the rule. The son of poor German immigrants, he spent ten years on Skid

Row in Los Angeles, working odd jobs by day and reading in public libraries by night. And he understood the nature of power better than almost anyone.

The worst thing about Karl Marx was not his personality or his hygiene. It was his socialist vision, which snared and doomed millions. He called the workers of the world to revolution, but, as the Italian writer Ignazio Silone put it, "Revolutions, like trees, must be judged by their fruit." Without exception, wherever Marx's socialist ideology found root, it grew into monstrous depravity. The regimes that attempted to put the rantings of this detestable lunatic into practice were responsible for a death toll of at least 100 million, according to *The Black Book of Communism*, the definitive scholarly look at the crimes of communism.

Some of Marx's disciples have attempted to explain this problem away with the old phrase "To make an omelet, you have to break a few eggs." The problem is, Marxists only break eggs; they never, *ever* make an omelet.

Marx professed to be "scientific," Paul Johnson writes, but in reality, "there was nothing scientific about him; indeed, in all that matters he was anti-scientific." He "never set foot in a mill, factory, mine or other industrial workplace in the whole of his life," turned down invitations to do so, and denounced fellow revolutionaries who did. Johnson adds that "Marx's fundamental failure to understand capitalism" arose "precisely because he was unscientific: he would not investigate the facts himself, or use objectively the facts investigated by others." All of Marx's work "reflects a disregard for truth which at times amounts to contempt."

And that, Johnson concludes, "is the primary reason why Marxism, as a system, cannot produce the results claimed for it."

Jesus warned us about people like Marx. In Matthew 7:15–17, he counseled: "Watch out for false prophets. They come to you in sheep's clothing, but inwardly they are ferocious wolves. By their fruit you will recognize them. Do people pick grapes from thornbushes, or figs from thistles? Likewise, every good tree bears good fruit, but a bad tree bears bad fruit."

Karl Marx was one rotten tree, inside and out.

Jesus was no socialist, and if he were preaching today, he would have nothing but disdain for Marx and his evil philosophy.

# 6

# THE GOLDEN RULE

For three hours, the famous "Stand in the Schoolhouse Door" riveted the country's attention. Alabama governor George Wallace blocked the entrance to Foster Auditorium at the University of Alabama in Tuscaloosa. His intent was to prevent two students from registering for classes. Why?

It had nothing to do with the content of their character and everything to do with the color of their skin. The students were African American.

On that tense day, June 11, 1963, President John F. Kennedy watched the scene on a black-and-white television in the White House. He had dispatched federal marshals and the deputy attorney general to ask Wallace to stand aside. When the governor refused, Kennedy issued an executive order to federalize the Alabama National Guard. Finally, Wallace backed down.

Relieved that the incident ended without violence, President Kennedy made a snap decision to speak to the nation about civil rights that very evening. Here's part of what he said:

The heart of the question is whether all Americans are to be afforded equal rights and equal opportunities, whether we are going to treat our fellow Americans as we want to be treated. If an American, because his skin is dark, cannot eat lunch in a restaurant open to the public, if he cannot send his children to the best public school available, if he cannot vote for the public officials who will represent him; if, in short, he cannot enjoy the full and free life which all of us want, then who among us would be content to have the color of his skin changed and stand in his place?

The president had invoked what philosophers call the "ethic of reciprocity," a moral principle—an *ideal*, actually—so universal that you can find it manifested in virtually every culture, religion, and ethical tradition. In Christianity it is known as the "Golden Rule." It's a concept that just about everybody everywhere will tell you they admire even when they don't live up to it.

## THE GOLDEN RULE AS AN IDEAL

Jesus himself spoke the Golden Rule, recorded in Luke 6:31 and Matthew 7:12: "So in everything, do to others what you would have them do to you, for this sums up the Law and the Prophets." He expressed it another way in Mark 12:28–34 when asked what the most important of all the commandments were. Second only to loving God, he said, was the commandment to "love your neighbor as yourself."

Human beings are not God, so we're far from perfect. We break commandments, as well as our own word. By our behavior, we sometimes make it difficult for other mortals to love us. Among us are a great many who lie, cheat, steal, and even assault the innocent. No significant faith or tradition suggests we are to ignore these evils or deny ourselves the right of self-defense against them. So again, think of the Golden Rule as an *ideal*—a lofty precept we should set our minds to.

The last six of the Ten Commandments are all extensions of the Golden Rule. These commandments deal with the individual's relationship to other individuals (after the first four involve the individual's relationship with God).

We are to honor our parents. We hope that our children will honor theirs.

We are to refrain from murder. We want others to regard life with the same respect.

We learn that adultery is wrong. We are grievously offended when someone else commits it with our spouse.

Commandments Eight through Ten warn against stealing, lying, and coveting. We don't like it when others steal from us, lie to us, or regard what's ours with an envious eye.

Wouldn't you want to live in a perfect world where everybody practices the Golden Rule all the time instead of just most of the time? What would such a world look like? It would be a world of peace and productivity. You could go about your business without fear that your life or possessions would be taken from you, because no one who might take them would want such a calamity to happen to them. No bullying, for any reason or purpose.

That puts a negative spin on the Golden Rule (*"don't do such-and-such"*), but there's also a positive side to it. If another person is sick or "down and out" in some other way, and you're in a position to help as a parent, relative, friend, or philanthropist, you would probably assist—in part because you'd want others to help you if you were in a similar situation, and in part because you might be instinctively sympathetic.

This is why the famous Samaritan who helped the man in need in Luke 10 is regarded universally as "Good." He came across an injured man and treated the person as he would want to be treated in such a situation. And he didn't force somebody else to help the man.

## MORALITY, LAW, AND ECONOMICS

Adam Smith, admired for his influential 1776 book, *The Wealth of Nations*, deserves just as much admiration for an earlier work, *The Theory of Moral Sentiments* (1759). In that book he postulated a version of the Golden Rule as a foundation for the evolution of generally accepted moral standards. As we enter adulthood and slowly jettison the exclusive focus of our infancy on "self," we begin to judge our personal behavior the way a third-party "impartial spectator" would.

Smith scholar James Otteson explained this point in a November 2000 article at FEE.org, "Adam Smith: Moral Philosopher":

We have all experienced the unpleasantness of being judged unfairly, that is, on the basis of biased or incomplete information (people who do not know our situation thinking poorly of us). This leads us to desire that others refrain from judging until they know the whole story; but because we all want this, our desire for mutual sympathy of sentiments subtly encourages us to adopt an outside perspective, as it were, in judging our own conduct.

That is, because we want others to be able to "enter into" our sentiments, we strive to moderate them to be what we think others will sympathize with; but we can only know what that is if we ask ourselves what the impartial observer would think. The voice of the impartial spectator becomes our second-nature guide of conduct. Indeed, Smith thinks it is what we call our "conscience."

Smith demonstrated, as Otteson puts it, that "a person's (largely unconscious) adoption of general rules, development of a conscience, and employment of the impartial spectator procedure are motivated by a fundamental, innate desire—the desire for mutual sympathy." That's the Golden Rule in action.

Standards of conduct do not originate in the laws of man. The most the law can do is recognize and uphold what men and women have come generally to accept through a spontaneous, organic process. As the nineteenth-century French economist and statesman Frédéric Bastiat wrote in *The Law*: "Life, liberty, and property do not exist because men have made laws. On the contrary, it was the fact that life, liberty, and property existed beforehand that caused men to make laws in the first place."

At the core of the moral universe is our innate desire for "mutual sympathy." Christians, and many people of other faiths as well, believe that God implants such sympathy as an element of our nature, but a belief in God is not necessary to accept the notion. You can be of another faith, or of no faith, and recognize that humans progress to the extent that they get along and work together for mutual benefit.

## SOCIALISM NULLIFIES THE GOLDEN RULE

Here we see another fundamental problem with socialism: it nullifies the Golden Rule.

Socialists proclaim "solidarity with the people." They say they only want to help others. The problem is how they seek to do it. If their plans stayed in the realm of helpful hints and requests for voluntary participation, they wouldn't be socialists. Capitalists invite and offer advice and participation all the time—with carrots, not sticks. If socialists actually help some people (and that is debatable), they do so only by hurting others.

The Golden Rule demands that we respect one another's differences, find common ground, and deal with one another voluntarily. It stresses a mutuality of benefit, as measured personally and subjectively by each party to an interaction. By its reliance on force, socialism tells us, "You're going to be drafted into this whether you like it or not, because we think it's good for you, or at least good for *somebody*."

By contrast, the very essence of a free marketplace is voluntary, mutually beneficial exchange. Though some small fraction of all trades may involve mistaken judgments, outright deception, or buyer's remorse, most transactions are wins for everybody. Each trader believes that what he's trading for is worth more to him than what he's giving up. This is true only when trades are entered into freely. If a party is forced to trade, he almost certainly believes he'll be worse off after the fact.

Compulsion is as incompatible with the Golden Rule as is fraud. In the marketplace, we offer one another something of value. If another party says, "No, thank you," we don't pull out a gun and demand that he trade. If we did, we wouldn't be doing to him what we would like him to do to us.

Some people think that because Jesus favored helping the less fortunate, he would support compulsion to do it. What a leap! He also favored eating, drinking, sleeping, washing, fasting, and praying—but he never remotely implied that those things required government programs, force, or taxation to pay for them.

I challenge anyone to find a passage in Scripture in which Jesus called on any government—Roman, Jewish, or another—to tax some and give to others as a method of assisting the needy.

## MEDDLERS, BUSYBODIES, AND HYPOCRITES

If you're a socialist, you need to ask yourself why you want to handle so many issues and problems at gunpoint. Why must everything require government? Where's your faith in and respect for your fellow citizens? You're so certain that forcing others to bend to your will is a good thing; would you mind if we turn the tables and do the same to you? If not, then why do you get to do these things but we don't?

Frédéric Bastiat stated the matter bluntly: "If the natural tendencies of mankind are so bad that it is not safe to permit people to be free, how is it that the tendencies of these organizers are always good? Do not the legislators and their appointed agents also belong to the human race? Or do they believe that they themselves are made of a finer clay than the rest of mankind?"

In 1 Peter 4:15, the apostle Peter addressed all believers with a message relevant to our examination of the Golden Rule. The NIV translation states, "If you suffer, it should not be as a murderer or thief or any other kind of criminal, or even as a meddler." The King James Version of this passage reads this way: "But let none of you suffer as a murderer, or as a thief, or as an evildoer, or as a busybody in other men's matters."

Take your pick: to be either a "meddler" or "a busybody in other men's matters" is to be disrespectful of another person's space. And that's incompatible with the Golden Rule.

Throughout the New Testament, we see appeals from Jesus as well as his disciples to focus on self-improvement. We are not to approach others as if *they're* flawed, *we're* perfect, and *we* know how to live *their* lives for them.

In Matthew 7:3–5, Jesus said:

Why do you look at the speck of sawdust in your brother's eye and pay no attention to the plank in your own eye? How can you say to your brother, "Let me take the speck out of your eye," when all the time there is a plank in your own eye? You hypocrite, first take the plank out of your own eye, and then you will see clearly to remove the speck from your brother's eye.

The Golden Rule is as golden as ever. It's just that some people think they have something better in mind for their fellow citizens.

# 7

# JESUS THE REDISTRIBUTIONIST?
# JESUS THE SOCIAL JUSTICE WARRIOR?

**"J**esus Was on the Side of the Poor and Exploited. Christian Politicians Should Remember That."

That headline appeared in London's *Guardian* newspaper shortly before Easter 2017. In the editorial that followed, Brad Chilcott, a pastor, wrote that Jesus "was overtly on the side of the poor, the excluded, the ignored, the disenfranchised, and the exploited," even when taking this position "damaged his reputation, his earning potential, and any hope he had of moving up the ranks of religious or political power."

I don't recall that Jesus expressed much concern for his "earning potential" or his place in "the ranks of religious or political power." But never mind that. Pastor Chilcott raised an issue that has become a huge part of the public debate: inequality. Just watch political campaigns. Questions about economic inequality receive "front-and-center emphasis," as the Gallup polling group observed in a 2019 report. So candidates compete to offer the most attractive plans to "fix" inequality.

And just as you're increasingly likely to hear that Jesus was a socialist, you're bound to hear politicians and pundits (and pastors like Chilcott) argue that Jesus opposed inequality because he was "on the side of the poor."

They often go further. To address inequality, they say, Jesus would endorse government programs to redistribute wealth.

Consider Pastor Chilcott again. He concluded, "Following Jesus requires we love people not only with words, theology, or charity but in costly solidarity." His editorial made clear that governments would need to impose this "costly solidarity." Chilcott called out the need for "laws," "national budgets," and "political policies" to correct the "economic, social, and cultural systems that perpetuate inequality, poverty, exclusion, and exploitation."

Of course, Jesus was concerned about the poor. The New Testament includes dozens of references to helping the poor and those who suffer from misfortune, oppression, or sickness. When, in Luke 4, he went to the synagogue in Nazareth, he read from the scroll of the prophet Isaiah: "The Spirit of the Lord is on me, because he has anointed me to proclaim good news to the poor." And in Luke 14, Jesus told a prominent Pharisee who had invited him into his home, "When you give a banquet, invite the poor, the crippled, the lame, the blind, and you will be blessed."

Does this mean Jesus would have favored government redistribution of wealth to erase inequality? Hardly.

Jesus more than recommended helping the poor; he declared that what one (especially a Christian) does to assist the deserving needy is an outward sign of the love for others that resides in one's heart.

"The poor you will always have with you, and you can help them any time you want," Jesus said in Matthew 26:11

and Mark 14:7. The key words there are *you can help* and *want to help*. He didn't say, "We're going to *make* you help whether you like it or not."

In justification of compulsory programs involving taxation, redistribution, and public welfare, we often hear the argument that "we are our brothers' keeper." This is a reference to the fourth chapter of Genesis in the Old Testament. Cain was jealous of the favor bestowed on his brother Abel, so he killed him. God spoke to Cain, asking him where Abel was. Cain's response in Genesis 4:9 began with a lie: "I don't know. *Am I my brother's keeper?*"

God's immediate reply was not, "Yes, you are!" Yet many Christians today hold to a vague understanding, often without knowing the original context of the phrase, that somewhere in the Bible, God mandates that we establish government-run welfare programs because we are to be "our brothers' keeper" through the political process.

Nonsense.

Here was God's actual reply to Cain: "What have you done? Listen! Your brother's blood cries out to me from the ground. Now you are under a curse and driven from the ground, which opened its mouth to receive your brother's blood from your hand. When you work the ground, it will no longer yield its crops for you. You will be a restless wanderer on the earth."

Search the New Testament and you will not find any passage that records Jesus using the "my brother's keeper" phrase. Of course, he preached love toward one another. He endorsed personal honesty and responsibility, especially to one's friends and families and contractual associates. But Jesus never called for anyone to abandon those responsibilities and hand them over to the state.

## THEFT

And yet socialist and many progressive policies demand that we hand responsibility over to the state. As we have seen, this approach *requires* government enforcement. But even if you remove government from the equation, you can see the trouble with using force to help others less fortunate.

Imagine a person who, acting entirely on his own initiative and exclusively from a desire to help the needy, decides to take from the rich and give every penny to the poor. This "poverty fighter" redistributes with no middleman—no bureaucracy, no paperwork, no vote buying, no deficits or debt, no cynical demagoguery. He gives the money to the poor who are close at hand, so he probably has a better sense of their needs than do distant government agents. All funds go directly to poverty relief, meaning that the poor receive more than they would if the original sum filtered through government.

Would this approach find approval from Jesus, his apostles, or anyone of authority in the early church?

If you've read the New Testament, you know the answer can't possibly be yes.

Why not?

Most important, the poverty fighter's actions spring from *theft*. No matter his intentions or where he puts the loot, nothing blesses theft. The Eighth Commandment categorically condemns theft, and Jesus never endorsed, condoned, or excused theft.

So neither this hypothetical poverty-fighting thief nor a government redirecting resources to the poor is remotely associated with the concern for others that Jesus encouraged.

## INDIVIDUALISM VS. COLLECTIVISM

Another problem with the fevered discussion about inequality lies in its focus on groups of people rather than individuals. Jesus did, of course, care about groups, whether it was the poor or believers or the Church. But at the core of his message, he stressed the value and uniqueness of individuals. Matters of salvation and character, for example, were always individual and never collective decisions.

In Luke 15:3–10, Jesus tells back-to-back parables that emphasize the critical value of the solitary individual:

> Then Jesus told them this parable: "Suppose one of you has a hundred sheep and loses one of them. Doesn't he leave the ninety-nine in the open country and go after the lost sheep until he finds it? And when he finds it, he joyfully puts it on his shoulders and goes home. Then he calls his friends and neighbors together and says, 'Rejoice with me; I have found my lost sheep.' I tell you that in the same way there will be more rejoicing in heaven over one sinner who repents than over ninety-nine righteous persons who do not need to repent.
>
> "Or suppose a woman has ten silver coins and loses one. Doesn't she light a lamp, sweep the house and search carefully until she finds it? And when she finds it, she calls her friends and neighbors together and says, 'Rejoice with me; I have found my lost coin.' In the same way, I tell you, there is rejoicing in the presence of the angels of God over one sinner who repents."

I'm appalled at the ease with which some people speak of their fellow citizens as though they are liquids to be homogenized or tools to be manipulated—not by request but by the force of political power. It's all for the nebulous collective good, they assure us, and they are often willing to do us harm if necessary to achieve it.

Alexis de Tocqueville, the great nineteenth-century observer of American life, would probably cringe at the rhetoric and policies of today's socialists and their progressive friends. When the Frenchman toured America in the early 1830s, he found that one of the country's strengths was that we focused on building things and people *up* instead of tearing either *down*. But Tocqueville offered a prescient warning:

> I have a passionate love for liberty, law, and respect for rights.... Liberty is my foremost passion. But one also finds in the human heart a depraved taste for equality, which impels the weak to want to bring the strong down to their level, and which reduces men to preferring equality in servitude to inequality in freedom.
>
> Equality is a slogan based on envy. It signifies in the heart of every republican: "Nobody is going to occupy a place higher than I."

Just as Tocqueville feared, the drive for equality has intensified.

## EQUAL OR FREE?

Here's a statement that I have used for decades: *Free people are not equal, and equal people are not free.*

Now, I am not talking about equality before the law. The law should apply to all people with impartiality. You, like everyone else, should be judged innocent or guilty based on whether you committed the crime, not on what color, sex, or creed you represent. This was the sense in which Thomas Jefferson meant those ringing words in the Declaration of Independence, "all men are created equal." No one is inferior to another in terms of his rights or his standing before God.

But socialists and a growing number of others call for a different kind of "equalness": equality in economic income or material wealth.

Economic equality in a free society is a mirage. All of us are different people. Our talents and abilities are not identical. We have different priorities. Some people work harder or work longer hours than others. So it should not come as a surprise that we earn different incomes.

And even if we all were magically made equal in wealth tonight, we'd be unequal in the morning because some of us would spend it and some of us would save it.

The fact that free people are not equal in economic terms is not to be lamented. Economic inequality, when it derives from the voluntary interaction of creative individuals and not from political power, testifies to the fact that people are being themselves, each putting his uniqueness to work in ways that fulfill him and provide value to others. As the French would say in a different context, *Vive la différence!*

People obsessed with economic equality do strange things. They become envious of others. They covet. They divide society into two piles: villains and victims. They spend far more time dragging someone else down than they do pulling themselves up. And if they make it to a legislature, they can do real harm. Then they not only call the cops—they *are* the cops.

To produce even a rough measure of economic equality requires government to force us all into such "equality." This is where government redistribution comes in, and where "taxing the hell" out of the rich comes in.

If economic inequality is an ailment, punishing effort and success is no cure. Coercive measures that aim to redistribute wealth prompt the smart or politically well-connected "haves" to seek refuge in havens here or abroad, while the hapless "have-nots" bear the full brunt of economic decline. A more productive expenditure of time would erase the intrusive government that ensures the "have-nots" become the "can-nots."

Paeans to the "common man" abound in literature, magazines, and political speeches. But I share a view expressed eloquently in "My Creed," which Dean Alfange, an immigrant from Turkey, wrote back in the 1920s:

> I do not choose to be a common man. It is my right to be uncommon—if I can. I seek opportunity—not security. I do not wish to be a kept citizen, humbled and dulled by having the state look after me.
>
> I want to take the calculated risk; to dream and to build, to fail and to succeed. I refuse to barter incentive for a dole. I prefer the challenges of life to the guaranteed existence; the thrill of fulfillment to the stale calm of utopia.
>
> I will not trade freedom for beneficence nor my dignity for a handout. I will never cower before any master nor bend to any threat. It is my heritage to stand erect, proud and unafraid; to think and act for myself, enjoy the benefit of my creations, and to face the world boldly and say, this I have done.

Indeed, *uncommon* people are the ones we should appreciate the most. I don't mean the uncommonly bad ones, but rather the uncommonly good ones—the sort that Jesus called us to be. Jesus never urged anyone to join the consensus, blend in with the crowd, or suborn himself to the "collective will." He never suggested that what's good or right is determined by what the majority wants, let alone by what any government declares. He never said to anyone: "Stop being exceptional. Be common." That is dehumanizing nonsense.

For these reasons, I am an unabashed proponent of *individualism* and a fierce opponent of *collectivism*. A collectivist sees humanity as a snowstorm, and that's as up-close as he gets if he is consistent. An individualist sees the storm, too, but immediately looks at the uniqueness of each snowflake that composes it.

The 1998 animated film *Antz* illustrates this point beautifully. The setting is an ant colony in which all ants behave as an obedient blob. This is convenient for the tyrant ants in charge. But a single ant shakes the debilitating collectivist mindset—and ultimately saves the colony through his individual initiative.

That ant, voiced by Woody Allen, takes action after an older ant, voiced by Danny Glover, dies in his arms, uttering these last words: "Don't make my mistake, kid. Don't follow orders your whole life. Think for yourself."

Being free to choose allows each of us to grow and develop, learn from our mistakes, and earn rewards for good judgment. Our choices shape who we are; they are expressions of our God-given individuality.

Individualism thereby embraces human nature. Collectivism attempts to thwart it. The largest, most horrendous mass murders in history arose from collectivist crusades against the individual. Joseph Stalin, responsible for a minimum of twenty million murders, is widely reputed to have declared, "A single death is a tragedy; a million deaths is a statistic."

The collectivist disparages the individual. He tells us that there is some higher moral good to "the group," especially if he gets to define it or run it. Collective entities invariably reduce to individuals telling other individuals what to do—*or else!* Socialism is profoundly collectivist. And because it relies on force, it's profoundly antisocial too.

As we have seen, attacks on the rich and crusades against income inequality reflect a sense of envy that pervades society. (Remember Tocqueville: "Equality is a slogan based on envy.") Businessman Jon Henschen explained this mindset in an October 2018 article for the website *Intellectual Takeout*: "This envy stems from a mentality that the economy is a finite pie and inequality results if someone gets a bigger slice of the economic pie. What many miss, however, is that the economy is not a finite pie, but thousands of pies, with inventors and entrepreneurs making new pies as they innovate, while obsolete pies fade away."

And the fact is that wealth creation is necessary to reducing poverty and distress. Serious economists who study where wealth comes from use terms like *entrepreneurship, investment, risk taking, division of labor, innovation, return on capital, customer service, incentives,* and so on. Socialists seem to have no theory of wealth creation; it is as if they think that wealth materializes magically just so they can redistribute it.

Again, the issue is not whether Jesus wanted us to help the poor. He most certainly did. But good intentions are not good enough. Jesus never signed on to political and economic policies that were compulsory or based on theft. Such policies would be immoral. That includes theft in the form of the forced redistribution of wealth.

In any case, redistribution policies have repeatedly proved to be ineffective at addressing poverty (as we will see in the next chapter). Socialists act as if they believe the poor are poor *because* the wealthy are wealthy. So they support policies that divide the wealth rather than creating more of it.

Obsessing over economic equality does not display compassion. When it's just an idea, it's bunk. When it's public policy, it's destructive. We waste our time vilifying the successful and slicing up the pie instead of baking a bigger one.

## SOCIAL JUSTICE

Tocqueville wrote that a "depraved taste for equality" drives "the weak to want to bring the strong down to their level." This leveling impulse animates the socialist idea. And it attracts many people because it comes across as "just" or "fair."

A particularly insidious notion making the news these days is "social justice." Not everyone who embraces it would call himself a socialist, but the rhetoric of social justice has become a core tactic of socialists. As my FEE colleague Jon Miltimore put it, they peddle a "softer, gentler version" of their program to eliminate inequality. Why? Because the "U.S. Constitution forbids the state from denying citizens 'equal protection of the laws,' so passing legislation that treats people differently is, well, tricky." The new, softer version of social justice "involves private companies and elite universities—versus the heavy hand of government—correcting 'imbalances' in wealth and privilege."

The social justice message has snookered many people, including some Christians. Social justice warriors position themselves on the side of the angels. They stand up for the "oppressed." They fight against racism and bigotry of all kinds. Columnist and author Jonah Goldberg put it well when he said, in a video for Prager University, that the term *social justice* is thrown around as shorthand for "'good things' no one needs to argue for and no one dare be against." The meaning of the term has become so fuzzy that social justice now "means anything its champions want it to mean," Goldberg added.

But it is important to understand what is involved here. Regardless of who or what forces the changes, implementing the social justice program will end up treating people not equally but *unequally*.

My friend Devin Foley, cofounder and CEO of *Intellectual Takeout*, has noted that what drives the social justice movement is "the belief that a just society cannot exist until all identity groups have parity with the others." Forget about individualism; this is pure collectivism. As Foley writes, "In such a system, we do not judge the individual based upon his actions, but rather we judge him based upon the identity group with which he is most associated." Social justice warriors sort out the "oppressors" from the "oppressed" and then "use collective action to lift up the oppressed and bring low the oppressors."

In the traditional view of justice, Foley explains, a person is judged based on his actions. According to that view, racism and bigotry are unjust because they judge an individual "by association rather than by the individual's actions."

Likewise, social justice condemns racism and bigotry. The problems arise in how social justice warriors try to right these wrongs. They "often commit the very evil they are attempting to erase," Foley says. They no longer judge an individual by his actions; they treat the individual "either well or poorly depending upon the identity group with which the individual is most associated."

For example, social justice warriors might condemn a white heterosexual male as racist not for any of his actions but simply because, centuries ago, members of his identity group established the American system of government. Since many social justice warriors assume that these institutions fostered systemic racism and homophobia, they see a white heterosexual male as benefiting from his "privilege." It doesn't matter whether the man realizes any of this. He remains part of the problem. In Foley's words: "Because his identity group is racist, he is racist."

By now it won't surprise you to learn that people invoke Jesus in defense of social justice. John Pavlovitz, a pastor and popular blogger, wrote an article in 2018 titled "Jesus Was a Social Justice Warrior." Another Christian blogger, Sierra White, the founder of the website *Ezer Rising*, went a step further in a 2019 post titled "Jesus—The First Social Justice Warrior."

But look closely at the basis for their claims. White began by asking: "Did Jesus speak out? Did he call out oppression, racism, and sexism?" She answered her own question: "Yes, yes he did." Here again we see social justice reduced to noble motives. The real question is, did Jesus follow the methods of today's social justice warriors? Absolutely not. White listed several episodes from the New Testament to show why Jesus was the "first social justice warrior." In none of those examples did he lump an individual into a certain identity group. Precisely the opposite was the case. Yes, as White noted, we repeatedly see Jesus "defend women, be kind and compassionate to those society treated as outcasts," and love people "who society didn't think He (a Jew) should even associate with (Galileans, Samaritans, diseased and possessed, sinners, etc.)." But that is because he recognized the God-given dignity and value of each *individual*.

Meanwhile, Pavlovitz justified his claim by saying that Jesus was a "compassionate caregiver and status quo changer," a "gentle healer and radical activist," a "wall-destroyer and barrier-breaker and least-lover." Jesus, Pavlovitz added, "poured out his life in acts of service and generosity and empathy and sacrifice."

He certainly did. But that did not make him a social justice warrior. Through his actions, Jesus embodied that all-important commandment to "love your neighbor as yourself." That commandment is a call to each of us—again, a call to character. It is not a call for government fiats or mass movements that blur each inherently unique individual into a faceless identity group.

In an essay in his book *Is God Happy?*, the great Polish philosopher Leszek Kołakowski—an outspoken critic of totalitarian socialism—condemned the "primitive social philosophy" that "proclaims not only that the common good of 'society' has priority over the interests of individuals, but that the very existence of individuals as persons is reducible to the existence of the social 'whole'; in other words, personal existence is, in a strange sense, unreal."

We would do well to remember Kołakowski's conclusion: "This is a convenient foundation for any ideology of slavery."

# 8

# WHAT IS REAL COMPASSION?

On October 10, 2019, a hero for the poor named Paul Polak passed away. The headline for his *New York Times* obituary read, "Paul Polak, Entrepreneur for Those Living on $2 a Day, Dies at 86." In more ways than one, this man's life teaches important lessons. Here's a portion of his *Times* obituary:

> In an era when foreign aid is largely based on charity, Dr. Polak instead advocated training people to earn livings by selling their neighbors basic necessities like clean water, charcoal, a ride in a donkey cart or enough electricity to charge a cellphone.
>
> Although the nonprofit companies he created did accept donations, their purpose was to help poor people make money. His target market was the 700 million people around the world surviving on less than $2 a day, and he traveled all over the world seeking them out.
>
> Before embarking on any project, Dr. Polak would interview dozens of villagers.

"I've interviewed over 3,000 families," he said in 2011. "I spend about six hours a day with each one— walking with them through their fields, asking them what they had for breakfast, how far their kids walk to school, what they feed their dog, what all their sources of income are. This is not rocket science. Any business-man knows this: You've got to talk to your customers."

His most successful project was in foot-powered treadle pumps to pull water out of the ground. Begin-ning in 1982, he sold millions for about $25 each in Ban-gladesh and India, he said. The company he created for the project, iDE for International Development Enter-prises, now operates in Asia, Africa and Latin America.

Paul Polak was a rich man when he died, one of the "one percent" that socialists tell us we should disdain and soak. Yet his efforts enriched the lives of untold millions on three continents. All that is a far cry from his humble beginnings.

Born into a Jewish family in Czechoslovakia in 1933, Polak grew up in a home that had no electricity or running water. His family fled the Nazi invasion in 1939, ending up in Canada. He managed to go to medical school and later prac-ticed psychiatry for twenty-three years. "For extra income," the *Times* obituary reported, "he bought and managed small apartment buildings, drilled for oil and invented an oil-well pump jack." He earned enough to give up his medical practice.

That allowed him to pursue his real passion in life: teaching the poor to be entrepreneurial. Polak belonged to the "teach a man to fish" school. But because his approach involved selling rather than charity—rather than "giving a man a fish"—he sometimes stood at odds with politicians, bureaucracies, and what he called "the establishment." He did not throw taxpayer money around. His solutions worked because they *had* to; it was *his* time and money he was investing in them.

The contrast between his approach and the government approach became vivid when he began selling his affordable treadle pumps. At the time, the World Bank was subsidizing expensive diesel pumps. The government-issued pumps "drew enough water to cover 40 acres," the *Times* reported. But the government agents who handed them out "could be bribed." The *Times* continued, "The richest landowner would thus become 'a waterlord,' who could drain the aquifer supplying everyone else's wells and then charge them for water."

Polak summed up the effects of this government program: "It was very destructive to social justice."

I read stories of enterprising people like Paul Polak and wonder, How much good for the poor would he have accomplished had he not pulled himself out of poverty and hardship? Or had the government, in the name of helping the poor, taxed away 90 percent of his income and laundered it through a welfare bureaucracy?

Perhaps the best question to ask is, *How do we get more Paul Polaks?*

## COMPASSION

Paul Polak helped far more poor people than many alleged poverty fighters do. He knew the long-term answer to poverty was wealth creation, not wealth redistribution. He never taxed anybody to do the job.

But the redistributionists are much more common than the Paul Polaks of the world.

The great majority of people who favor redistribution are no doubt well intentioned. They really do want to help the needy, and many of them believe the welfare state comports with Christian principles. To them, favoring these government programs expresses true compassion.

Are they right?

Jesus clearly holds that compassion is a wholesome value to possess, but I know of no passage anywhere in the New Testament that suggests it's a value he would impose at gunpoint. Christians are commanded to love, to pray, to be kind, to serve, to forgive, to be truthful, to worship the one God, to learn and grow in both spirit and character. All those things are to be personal. They must come from the heart. They require no politicians, police, bureaucrats, or government programs.

True compassion is a bulwark of strong families and communities, of liberty and self-reliance. False compassion—which employs compulsion—is fraught with danger and produces dubious results. True compassion manifests itself when people help others out of a genuine sense of caring and brotherhood. (Think once more of the Good Samaritan.) It is not asking your legislator or congressman to do it for you. True compassion comes from your heart, not from the state or federal treasury. True compassion is a deeply personal thing, not a check from a distant bureaucracy—one that puts an involuntary burden on someone else.

As Marvin Olasky pointed out in his book *The Tragedy of American Compassion*, *The Oxford English Dictionary* gives the following as the original definition of *compassion*: "suffering together with another, participation in suffering." Similarly, Noah Webster, in the 1834 edition of his *American Dictionary of the English Language*, defined compassion as "a suffering with another." The word itself points to this definition: *com* means "with," and *passion*, from the Latin term *pati*, means "to suffer." This understanding of compassion emphasizes personal involvement with the needy, suffering *with* them, not just giving to them.

The way many people, especially socialists and progressives, use *compassion* today corrupts the original meaning of the word. They regard compassion as little more than (in Olasky's words) "the feeling, or emotion, when a person is moved by the suffering or distress of another, and by the desire to relieve it." There is a world of difference between those two definitions. One demands personal action; the other is simply a "feeling," one that usually leads to a call for someone else— namely, government—to deal with the problem. One describes a Red Cross volunteer; the other describes the demagogue who gives away little of his own resources but lots of yours.

## PASSING THE BUCK

The plain fact is that government compassion is not the same as personal and private compassion. So it is a mistake to use a person's willingness to spend government funds on aid programs as the gauge of his compassion. Professor William B. Irvine of Wright State University explained why:

> It would be absurd to take a person's willingness to increase defense spending as evidence that the person is himself brave, or to take a person's willingness to spend government money on athletic programs as evidence that the person is himself physically fit. In the same way as it is possible for a "couch potato" to favor government

funding of athletic teams, it is possible for a person who lacks compassion to favor various government aid programs. Conversely, it is possible for a compassionate person to oppose these programs.

Professor Irvine said that if you want to determine how compassionate an individual is, you are wasting your time if you ask for whom he voted. Instead, you should ask what charitable contributions he has made and whether he has done any volunteer work lately. You might also inquire into how he responds to the needs of his relatives, friends, and neighbors.

Many of the political world's most boisterous welfare statists display little true generosity. Whereas small-government conservatives and libertarians tend to give generously from their own pockets, socialists and progressives are notorious cheapskates with regard to charity. (For a mountain of evidence in that regard, see the 2006 book *Who Really Cares* by Arthur Brooks, then a professor at Syracuse University and later president of the American Enterprise Institute.)

Christianity is not about passing the buck to government when it comes to relieving the plight of the poor. Caring for them—which means helping them *overcome* poverty, not making them dependent on the state—has been an essential fact in the life of a true Christian for two thousand years. It is a voluntary response to having received God's grace. It's a personal choice to get involved, to give of yourself.

But don't take my word for it. Consider what the apostle Paul said in 2 Corinthians 9:7: "Each of you should give what you have decided in your heart to give, not reluctantly or under compulsion, for God loves a cheerful giver."

Throughout his extensive journeys, Paul practiced what he preached, pitching in to assist the deserving needy. In

Acts 20:34–35, he said: "You yourselves know that these hands of mine have supplied my own needs and the needs of my companions. In everything I did, I showed you that by this kind of hard work we must help the weak, remembering the words the Lord Jesus himself said: 'It is more blessed to give than to receive.'" He offered himself as an example to his fellow Christians, but he never *mandated* that they help the poor. His words in 2 Corinthians 8:8 are plain and simple: "I am not commanding you, but I want to test the sincerity of your love by comparing it with the earnestness of others."

Later, in 2 Corinthians 8:24, Paul implored his audience to give freely because that was the way others would know that it came from the heart: "Show these men the proof of your love and the reason for our pride in you, so that the churches can see it."

Cato Institute senior fellow Doug Bandow, in his book *Beyond Good Intentions: A Biblical View of Politics*, noted the significance of Paul's "cheerful giver" by asking this question: "If Paul was not willing to command believers in a church that he had founded to help their less fortunate Christian brethren, would he have advocated that the civil authorities tax unbelievers for the same purpose?"

Of course not. Nothing in the New Testament suggests that Paul either called for or would support compulsory, socialistic, or welfare-state measures. This was the same Paul, by the way, who said that the able-bodied needy owed something to their charitable brothers. In 2 Thessalonians 3:7–10, he wrote: "We were not idle when we were with you, nor did we eat anyone's food without paying for it. On the contrary, we worked night and day, laboring and toiling so that we would not be a burden to any of you.... We gave you this rule: 'The one who is unwilling to work shall not eat.'"

Once again, we see that Jesus, Paul, and other early Christian leaders were calling for an inner renaissance of *character*, one individual at a time, from the heart and not by force. Good character embodies many traits and virtues, including empathy for the less fortunate, a desire to see them flourish.

## THE FAILURES OF THE WAR ON POVERTY

There is another reason support for government programs can't be mistaken for compassion: those programs simply aren't as effective at helping the needy as are private efforts. When we expect the government to substitute for what we ought to do, we expect the impossible and end up with the intolerable. We don't really solve problems; we just manage them expensively into perpetuity and create a bunch of new ones along the way.

Economists have demonstrated time and again that the so-called War on Poverty, which began in the mid-1960s, didn't accomplish what its advocates promised. Not at all. America's poverty rate had actually declined significantly *before* the federal government declared "war" on poverty. But after the War on Poverty began, the poverty rate hardly changed. This despite the fact that the federal government has poured staggering sums of taxpayer dollars into anti-poverty programs.

Consider: In its first half century, the War on Poverty cost more than $22 trillion (in constant 2012 dollars). That's more than triple what the United States had spent on all the military wars in its history *combined*. (See Daniel J. Mitchell's data-filled article at FEE.org, "Poverty in the U.S. Was Plummeting—Until Lyndon Johnson Declared War on It," as well as the Heritage Foundation's 2014 report "The War on Poverty After 50 Years.")

In 1996, President Bill Clinton signed welfare reform into law. By that point, total government welfare spending had risen from just over 1 percent of gross domestic product in 1965 to well over 5 percent of GDP—higher than the record set during the Great Depression. But the poverty rate remained *almost exactly* where it had been in 1965. In effect, taxpayers paid poor people to stay poor, so they did.

By the time welfare reform passed, many people—including Bill Clinton—recognized that millions of Americans on welfare were living lives of demoralizing dependency, that the system rewarded families for breaking up, and that the number of children born out of wedlock had reached stratospheric levels. "Compassionate" government programs played a major role in exacerbating these terrible developments.

### "SHUN THE BAIT"

OK, you say, maybe we should avoid big-government social programs that simply send checks to the poor. Instead, let's have the government "privatize" welfare by giving the money to church-based charities and let them do the job. This is reminiscent of President George W. Bush's "faith-based initiative" of 2001, a well-intentioned proposal that combined government funding with the private, voluntary sector.

President Bush was right to recognize the fruitful role of America's private, faith-based "armies of compassion." For many reasons, such groups are far more effective in solving social problems—poverty, homelessness, illiteracy, to name a few—than are government programs and bureaucracies. They treat the whole person, which means they get to the root of problems, often including spiritual, attitudinal, and behavioral deficiencies. They demand accountability, which means they don't simply hand over a check every two weeks without expecting the needy to do much in return or to change destructive patterns of behavior. And if these groups don't produce results, they wither; the parishioners or others who voluntarily support them will put their mites elsewhere.

When a government program fails to perform, its lobbyists make a case for more money, and they usually get it. Every day, tens of thousands of faith-based organizations, large and small, demonstrate the point that management expert Peter Drucker made about how to address social problems: "The nonprofits spend far less for results than governments spend for failure."

In a single pithy question, John Fund, then of the *Wall Street Journal*, underscored Americans' instinctive regard for private aid, no matter what they may say in public: "If you had a financial windfall and wanted to help the poor, would you even think about giving time or a check to the government?" Millions of Americans give to the Red Cross and the Salvation Army; almost nobody writes checks to the welfare department—not even socialists.

The problem with the Bush proposal was not, as some critics argued, that it put faith in a position to corrupt the government. All the ingredients necessary for corruption in government were already there: vast sums of other people's money and far more power than any government should ever have.

The real problem was that the president's initiative *put government in a position to corrupt faith.* One reason related to the relentlessly secular nature of the modern American state.

Another issue was that the federal program put churches at risk of becoming dependent on the state's largesse. More than a few people of faith—who would ordinarily be the first to argue that God doesn't need federal funds to do his work— lined up to try to secure funding through the Bush program.

Such corruption is exactly what happened in the Roman Empire. After years of being shunned and persecuted, Christians suddenly enjoyed the official blessing of the Roman state when Emperor Constantine came to power in A.D. 324. For the first time, the empire subsidized priests, churches, and their good works. Christians emerged from hiding in Rome's catacombs to partake of the state's support.

Soon the church depended on the empire's financial aid. In 361, Emperor Julian launched a backlash against state-supported Christian influence. By withdrawing financial support, he crippled the church. He even forbade Christians from teaching in the schools. For the sake of both their faith and Roman society at large, the Christians of the fourth century should have remained pure and independent—advice the poet John Dryden expressed thirteen centuries later: "And better shun the bait, than struggle in the snare."

But the primary problem with a federal faith-based initiative lay in the very nature of government. Resting as it does on the compulsory tax power, government funding of any kind conflicts with the very thing that makes private, faith-based programs work: *charitable impulses that are voluntary and inner-motivated.*

From start to finish, what private charities do is a manifestation of free will. No one is compelled to provide assistance. No one is coerced to pay for it. No one is required to accept it. All parties come together of their own volition. That's the magic of it.

The link connecting the giver, the provider, and the receiver is strong precisely because each knows he can walk away at the slightest hint of insincerity, broken promises, or poor performance. Because each party gives of his own time or resources voluntarily, he tends to focus on the mission at hand and doesn't get bogged down in other agendas, like filling out the proper paperwork or currying favor with politicians.

And if we have learned anything from history's welfare states, it is that they didn't resolve the problem of poverty— and worse, they created plenty of new problems. The poor are still with us. The welfare state empowers greedy, myopic politicians; breeds corruption; undermines the work ethic; fosters dependency and family breakup; and crowds out more effective private initiatives. It mortgages the future, economically and spiritually. From every vantage point, it's the antithesis of good character.

Historically, few things appear more risky than a massive welfare state. It has put more than a few countries out of business. But no nation ever died because of an overabundance of character.

There are far better ways to reduce poverty than through plunder, legal or illegal. Free markets, private property, rule of law, entrepreneurship, wealth creation, personal responsibility, and voluntary charity come to mind—and the use of government force crowds out all of those.

Almost everybody wants to help those in need. The crucial question is *how* to help. Let's not make the mistake of arguing that to use force, plunder, and dependency is somehow "the Christian thing to do."

# 9

# HUMILITY

More than 1,600 years ago, a remarkable man wrote a small book titled *Our Lord's Sermon on the Mount*. He is known in history as Augustine of Hippo. His book opened with these words: "If anyone will piously and soberly consider the sermon which our Lord Jesus Christ spoke on the mount, as we read it in the Gospel according to Matthew, I think that he will find in it, so far as regards the highest morals, a perfect standard of the Christian life."

Few Christians would disagree with Augustine's assessment. The sermon, delivered early in Jesus's ministry, is his longest uninterrupted statement. It comprises three chapters of the Book of Matthew (5, 6, and 7) and is referenced or excerpted elsewhere in the New Testament as well. It includes the well-known Beatitudes and the Lord's Prayer. It is a gold mine of advice for leading a Christian life.

Augustine is an interesting story, by the way. As the decadent Roman Empire crumbled around him and barbarian invaders sacked the Eternal City, Augustine's defense of

Christianity didn't waver for a second. A giant of Western thought and Christian doctrine, he was more than a little skeptical of earthly political power. In his classic *City of God*, he wrote:

> The dominion of bad men is hurtful chiefly to themselves who rule, for they destroy their own souls by greater license in wickedness; while those who are put under them in service are not hurt except by their own iniquity. For to the just all the evils imposed on them by unjust rulers are not the punishment of crime, but the test of virtue. The good man, though a slave, is free; the wicked, though he reigns, is a slave, and not the slave of a single man, but—what is worse—the slave of as many masters as he has vices.

Augustine did not believe that the possession of earthly power granted you some special abilities to plan the lives of others. It didn't occur to him that legislation or decrees should pass unquestioned. "An unjust law is no law at all," he maintained. To him, government was at best a necessary evil, one that grew more threatening the bigger it became. In this passage from *City of God*, he questioned the legitimacy of government itself:

> Justice being taken away, then, what are kingdoms but great robberies? For what are robberies themselves, but little kingdoms? The band itself is made up of men; it is ruled by the authority of a prince; it is knit together by the pact of the confederacy; the booty is divided by the law agreed on. If, by the admittance of abandoned men, this evil increases to such a degree that it holds places,

fixes abodes, takes possession of cities, and subdues peoples, it assumes the more plainly the name of a kingdom, because the reality is now manifestly conferred on it, not by the removal of covetousness, but by the addition of impunity. Indeed, that was an apt and true reply which was given to Alexander the Great by a pirate who had been seized. For when that king had asked the man what he meant by keeping hostile possession of the sea, he answered with bold pride, "What thou meanest by seizing the whole earth; but because I do it with a petty ship, I am called a robber, whilst thou who dost it with a great fleet art styled emperor."

Augustine was a man of peace. He urged Christians to engage only in voluntary interactions with themselves and others unless and until a grave wrong required force to stop violence. His was, in effect, an early case for *self-defense* and for a concept now known as the nonaggression principle. That ethical pillar posits that one should not *initiate* force or violence against the person or property of another. I doubt very much that Augustine would approve of legal plunder by the state as compatible with core Christian principles of brotherhood, justice, and nonviolence.

Of all the virtues of personal character, Augustine reserved the highest praise for one that's often overlooked in our times: *humility*. We may define it as the absence of arrogance or false pride, a modest view of ourselves that takes into account our shortcomings. It's a recognition of the knowledge we don't know, the imperfections we all endure, the self-improvement we have yet to achieve.

"Humility," Augustine asserted, "is the foundation of all the other virtues; hence, in the soul in which this virtue does not exist there cannot be any other virtue except in mere appearance." Elsewhere, he put it this way: "If you plan to build a tall house of virtues, you must first lay deep foundations of humility."

No wonder Augustine thought so highly of the Sermon on the Mount. Humility is the sermon's core theme, even as Jesus offered instruction or commentary in many other areas.

And humility is a virtue that challenges the very core of the socialist agenda.

## "THE SPIRIT WHICH PUFFS UP"

The Sermon on the Mount opens with a powerful statement about those who possess it, the first of eight Beatitudes: "Blessed are the poor in spirit, for theirs is the kingdom of heaven."

Note the difference from the Sermon on the Plain in Luke 6:20 (discussed in chapter 3 of this book). Here, in Matthew, Jesus did not say, "Blessed are the poor in income and material things." He wasn't praising poverty. Those two words "in spirit" show that he was talking about something different. Augustine explained to whom Jesus referred: "The poor in spirit are rightly understood here as meaning the humble and God-fearing, that is, those who have not the spirit which puffs up."

*Those who have not the spirit which puffs up.* Stop and think about that. A person who is "puffed up" is supremely sure of himself, condescending toward others, and often intolerant of people who want to go their own way. Augustine asked rhetorically, "Who does not know that the proud are spoken of as puffed up, as if swelled out with wind?"

Jesus returned to humility later in the Sermon on the Mount, when he warned against a public show of one's "righteousness." Such affectations are a form of puffery, designed to shine a light on oneself. They detract from the sincerity of the act. "So when you give to the needy," Jesus said by way of example, "do not announce it with trumpets, as the hypocrites do in the synagogues and on the streets, to be honored by others." Jesus applied the same principle to prayer and fasting. He urged believers to avoid imitating "the hypocrites" who loved to pray on street corners or flaunt their hunger so they could "be seen by others."

The apostle Paul offered a similar warning in Romans 12:3. Urging humility, he said, "For by the grace given me I say to every one of you: Do not think of yourself more highly than you ought, but rather think of yourself with sober judgment, in accordance with the faith God has distributed to each of you."

C. S. Lewis, the great novelist and Christian apologist, observed the dangers of pride and puffery: "A proud man is always looking down on things and people; and, of course, as long as you are looking down, you cannot see something that is above you." Jesus pointed us another way. In his first Beatitude, he said that those of a humble nature—who eschew vanity, presumption, narcissism, and an overblown sense of their abilities—will be happy.

Yet a lot of people display excessive pride. The world of politics and government attracts more than its fair share. No group along the political spectrum has a monopoly on puffery. But the very essence of socialism requires a confidence that you really do know what is best for others.

Just listen to political candidates who label themselves socialist or "democratic socialist" or even progressive. They have a plan for everything. Their plans dictate what you can and can't do. Their litany of compulsory *this* and mandatory *that* is staggering.

Take Bernie Sanders, America's most influential democratic socialist. The word *transform* became central to his 2020 presidential candidacy. A single policy brief on his campaign website used *transform* or *transformation* fourteen times. The candidate promised to "transform our energy system," "transform our transportation sector," and "transform our agricultural sector." But all those were means to the larger end: "a wholesale transformation of our society." That transformation must come through programs and edicts from on high.

In October 2019, Sanders offered this frightening boast on social media: "When we win, we are going to fundamentally change the nature of the presidency. I will not only be commander-in-chief, but organizer-in-chief." Remember, "organizing" doesn't come in the form of friendly tips and suggestions; *he* will "organize," and *you* will be "organized," whether you like it or not.

In the 2016 campaign, Sanders railed against "millionaires and billionaires." But later he was forced to admit that he was a millionaire himself. Perhaps not coincidentally, in the 2020 race, Sanders nearly stopped mentioning millionaires. CNBC reporter Jacob Pramuk documented the change by reviewing debate transcripts and Sanders's social media posts.

Another prominent democratic socialist, Congresswoman Alexandria Ocasio-Cortez, drew national attention in 2019 for sponsoring legislation for a "Green New Deal." This sweeping plan took aim at not only climate change but also "systemic racial, regional, social, environmental, and economic injustices." The legislation called for "a new national, social, industrial, and economic mobilization on a scale not seen since World War II and the New Deal."

There was nothing humble about Ocasio-Cortez's all-encompassing plan. It was full of proposed orders that encompassed even the nitty-gritty of retrofitting *your* house with *her* environmental gimmicks. The plan laid out which technologies should be suppressed and which ones should be subsidized. As if any politician, even one surrounded by a cadre of experts, can just *know* exactly what needs to be done and what the consequences of the plan will be.

This is the arrogance of planners.

## THE "WHOLESALE TRANSFORMATION OF OUR SOCIETY"?

T. S. Eliot said, "Humility is the most difficult of all virtues to achieve; nothing dies harder than the desire to think well of oneself." In a similar vein, an old Mac Davis tune proclaimed, "Oh Lord, it's hard to be humble!"

This goes for all of us. We are human, after all. But even a modest dose of humility might open the eyes of socialists and progressives to the ugly record of concentrated power. Socialism's historical record of failure is undeniable. Somehow socialists assume that *this time*—with them or their friends in charge—things will turn out differently. Their good intentions will make them exceptional.

This is the antithesis of humility.

To be humble is to understand how little you really know. Socrates, surely one of the wisest people who ever lived, said, "I know that I have no wisdom, small or great." This was not false modesty. Socrates understood that he was wise only to the extent he recognized that "the wisdom of men is worth little or nothing," for "God only is wise."

Humility doesn't mean running yourself down. It means

cultivating a healthy sense of your limitations so you can recognize the vast room you have to grow and improve. It means
not presuming to know more than you do.

Leonard E. Read, the founder of the organization I later led
for nearly eleven years—the Foundation for Economic Education (FEE)—wrote a famous essay in 1958 called "I, Pencil."
It underscores the necessity of humility in a way that I can't
help but think even Jesus would admire. Let me summarize
it for you here: *No one person—repeat, no one, no matter how
smart or how many degrees follow his name—could create
from scratch, entirely by himself, a small, everyday pencil, let
alone a car or an airplane.*

A mere pencil—such a simple thing, yet it's beyond any
one person's complete comprehension. Think of all that went
into making and selling it, the countless people and skills
assembled miraculously in the marketplace without a single
mastermind—indeed, without anyone knowing more than
a small part of the whole process. If you were assigned the
task of creating a pencil entirely from scratch, on your own,
you would have to learn and apply the skills of an engineer, a
miner, a logger, a machinist, and dozens of others whose work
goes into pencil making.

You couldn't do it. No one could. And yet without any
central plans or politicians, pencils materialize by the billions
every year. What does that say about the ability of any one
person or group of people to plan an economy of several hundred million people? The implications of this lesson for the
economy and the role of government are huge.

Read's message pricks the inflated egos of those who
think they know how to mind everybody else's business. It
explains in plain language why central planning of society or
an economy is an exercise in arrogance and futility. If I can't

make something as simple as a pencil, I had better be careful about how smart I think I am!

We would miss a large implication of Leonard Read's message, and that of Jesus, too, if we concluded that error begins only when the planners plan big. Error begins the moment one tosses humility aside, assumes he knows the unknowable, and employs the force of government to control more and more of other people's lives.

But history is littered with people who ignore this lesson. Call them what you will—socialist, progressive, collectivist, statist, interventionist—they come up with grand (and presumptuous) plans for rearranging society to fit their vision of the common good, plans that not only fail but also kill or impoverish people in the process.

None of the socialists of the world know how to make a pencil, yet they want to remake entire societies. What could possibly go wrong?

# 10

# TWO THEOLOGIANS WHO GOT IT RIGHT

I am not a theologian by profession. I am an economist and a historian who happens to be a Christian. Although I have read the Bible from beginning to end several times and parts of it dozens of times, a reader might nonetheless want more "authoritative" analysis, at least with regard to my assertions about Jesus and socialism.

One who studies, interprets, and offers commentary on the Bible as his or her full-time profession would properly be termed a theologian. He may or may not choose to delve into how Scripture applies to the world of contemporary politics, economics, and social conditions. Those theologians who do are not unanimous on every point, to say the least. Some might assert that Jesus was indeed a socialist. Obviously I believe them to be profoundly mistaken, however well intentioned.

In the twentieth century, two theologians who I believe "got it right" were C. S. Lewis and J. Gresham Machen. Because their views influenced my own considerably, I want the reader to know more about them.

## C. S. LEWIS

"Friendship," wrote C. S. Lewis in a December 1935 letter, "is the greatest of worldly goods. Certainly to me it is the chief happiness of life. If I had to give a piece of advice to a young man about a place to live, I think I should say, 'sacrifice almost everything to live where you can be near your friends.'"

Clive Staples Lewis (1898–1963) was the sort of person I would give an arm to have as a friend across the street. I can only imagine the thrill of listening to him for hours on end. This distinguished scholar and thinker was a prolific author of works in Christian apologetics and of the seven-part children's fantasy *The Chronicles of Narnia*. Those novels have sold more than 100 million copies and have been adapted into major motion pictures.

But Lewis was not merely a novelist. Many regard him as the greatest lay theologian of the twentieth century. While teaching literature first at Oxford and then at Cambridge, Lewis wrote more than twenty nonfiction books, including *Mere Christianity* and *The Abolition of Man*, plus hundreds of speeches, essays, letters, and radio addresses. His influence, substantial while he was alive, may be even greater in the world today.

Stacked against his literary and theological offerings, Lewis's commentary on political and economic matters is comparatively slim—mostly a few paragraphs scattered here and there, not in a single volume. Lewis scholars have examined those snippets to discern where he might land on the political spectrum. Was he a socialist, a classical liberal, an anarchist, a minarchist, a theocrat, or something else?

I believe Lewis might be perfectly happy to be labeled a Christian libertarian. He embraced minimal government because he had no illusions about the essentially corrupt nature of man and the inevitable magnification of corruption when it's mixed with political power. He knew that virtuous character proved indispensable to a happy life, personal fulfillment, and societal progress—and that it must come not by the commands of political elites but from the growth and consciences of each individual, one at a time. He celebrated civil society and peaceful cooperation and detested the presumptuous arrogance of officialdom.

His 1958 essay "Willing Slaves of the Welfare State" is a gold mine of insights about government and its proper relationship to the individual. As the title suggests, Lewis condemned the rapid rise of big government around the world. He did not have in mind only the totalitarian regimes the Allies had defeated in the Second World War. He lamented the situation that had arisen "in most modern communities." Lewis wrote: "Two wars necessitated vast curtailments of liberty, and we have grown, though grumblingly, accustomed to our chains. The increasing complexity and precariousness of our economic life have forced Government to take over many spheres of activity once left to choice or chance."

Lewis saw little hope in turning back the rise of the state. "Probably we cannot, certainly we shall not, retrace our steps," he wrote. More than sixty years later, we still hear a chorus of politicians and bureaucrats calling for greater interference in our liberties and in markets. Lewis explained the source of this ever-present danger:

> The modern State exists not to protect our rights but to do us good or make us good—anyway, to do something to us or to make us something. Hence the new name "leaders" for those who were once "rulers." We are less their

subjects than their wards, pupils, or domestic animals. There is nothing left of which we can say to them, "Mind your own business." Our whole lives are their business.

Lewis specifically cited Christianity as a key source of the "classical political theory" he now proclaimed dead—killed by the modern state. He saw through the promises of the socialists and welfare statists who (much like the progressives of today) presented government programs as the solution to man's problems. In opposition to their calls for more and bigger government programs, he presented a better way— *freedom*:

> I believe a man is happier, and happy in a richer way, if he has "the freeborn mind." But I doubt whether he can have this without economic independence, which the new society is abolishing. For economic independence allows an education not controlled by Government; and in adult life it is the man who needs, and asks, nothing of Government who can criticize its acts and snap his fingers at its ideology. Read Montaigne; that's the voice of a man with his legs under his own table, eating the mutton and turnips raised on his own land. Who will talk like that when the State is everyone's schoolmaster and employer?

In one of my favorite passages, Lewis wrote:

> To live his life in his own way, to call his house his castle, to enjoy the fruits of his own labor, to educate his children as his conscience directs, to save for their prosperity after his death—these are wishes deeply ingrained in

civilized man. Their realization is almost as necessary to our virtues as to our happiness. From their total frustration disastrous results both moral and psychological might follow.

Throughout the essay, Lewis expressed his disdain for the "pretensions" of the state, "the grounds on which it demands my obedience." In every age, he wrote, "the men who want us under their thumb" will advance the particular myths and prejudices of the day so they can "cash in" on hopes and fears. That, he said, opens the door to tyranny in one form or another.

Lewis posed a question that all of us today should consider as progressives tempt us with promises of what the state can do for us—"free" healthcare, "free" college, "free" child care, and so much more: "The question about progress has become the question whether we can discover any way of submitting to the worldwide paternalism of a technocracy without losing all personal privacy and independence. Is there any possibility of getting the super Welfare State's honey and avoiding the sting?"

Lewis understood human nature and the corrupting influence of power. He concluded his essay with a powerful reflection on why it is delusional to believe that the welfare state will take good care of us:

What assurance have we that our masters will or can keep the promise which induced us to sell ourselves?... All that can really happen is that some men will take charge of the destiny of the others. They will be simply men; none perfect; some greedy, cruel and dishonest. The more completely we are planned the more powerful they will be. Have we discovered some new reason why, this time, power should not corrupt as it has done before?

Lewis also conveyed this understanding of human nature in an essay that was published after his death, in the collection *Of Other Worlds* (1966). In the essay, he wrote:

Being a democrat, I am opposed to all very drastic and sudden changes of society (in whatever direction) because they never in fact take place except by a particular technique. That technique involves the seizure of power by a small, highly disciplined group of people; the terror and the secret police follow, it would seem, automatically. I do not think any group good enough to have such power. They are men of like passions with ourselves. The secrecy and discipline of their organization will have already inflamed in them that passion for the inner ring which I think at least as corrupting as avarice; and their high ideological pretensions will have lent all their passions the dangerous prestige of the Cause. Hence, in whatever direction the change is made, it is for me damned by its modus operandi. The worst of all public dangers is the committee of public safety.

In a 1943 essay, "Equality," Lewis offered further reflections on how the state gathers power. Lewis believed that men and women should be equal before the law, but he believed just as firmly that the law should not aim to make people equal in *outcomes*, such as in material wealth. To achieve such "equality" would require ugly force.

Lewis warned against trying to achieve economic equality

as an "ideal." When we do that, he said, "we begin to breed that stunted and envious sort of mind which hates all superiority." He continued: "That mind is the special disease of democracy, as cruelty and servility are the special diseases of privileged societies. It will kill us all if it grows unchecked."

His suspicions of trying to enforce equality also come through in *The Screwtape Letters* (1942), one of his most popular satirical pieces. Lewis wrote the novel as a series of missives from a senior demon, named Screwtape, to his nephew Wormwood, who carries the official title of Junior Tempter. Screwtape is training Wormwood in how to corrupt mankind, to turn society into a hell on earth. It's very revealing of Lewis's political thinking that the senior demon instructs his pupil to "equalize" and "democratize" to achieve their nefarious objectives:

What I want to fix your attention on is the vast, overall movement toward the discrediting, and finally elimina tion, of every kind of human excellence—moral, cul tural, social, or intellectual. And is it not pretty to notice how Democracy is now doing for us the work that once was done by the ancient Dictatorships, and by the same methods? . . . Allow no pre-eminence among your subjects. Let no man live who is wiser, or better, or more famous, or even handsomer than the mass. Cut them down to a level; all slaves, all ciphers, all nobodies. All equals. Thus Tyrants could practice, in a sense, "democracy." But now "democracy" can do the same work without any other tyranny than her own.

If the deeply Christian Lewis had been a socialist of any persuasion, I don't see how he could have written any of the above. He never glorified the ambitions of central planners. On the contrary, he criticized the pomposity of politicians. In the 1960 essay "The World's Last Night," he wrote: "The higher the pretensions of our rulers are, the more meddlesome and impertinent their rule is likely to be and the more the thing in whose name they rule will be defiled.... Let our masters...leave us some region where the spontaneous, the unmarketable, the utterly private, can still exist."

If I had to choose a favorite among Lewis's pithy putdowns of big government, it would be this excerpt from his 1949 essay "The Humanitarian Theory of Punishment":

> Of all tyrannies a tyranny sincerely exercised for the good of its victims may be the most oppressive. It may be better to live under robber barons than under omnipotent moral busybodies. The robber baron's cruelty may sometimes sleep, his cupidity may at some point be satiated; but those who torment us for our own good will torment us without end for they do so with the approval of their own conscience. They may be more likely to go to Heaven yet at the same time likelier to make a Hell of earth. This very kindness stings with intolerable insult. To be "cured" against one's will and cured of states which we may not regard as disease is to be put on a level of those who have not yet reached the age of reason or those who never will; to be classed with infants, imbeciles, and domestic animals.

Lewis couldn't bring himself to look on government as God, a substitute for God, or a reasonable facsimile of God. Government was composed of imperfect mortals. That meant it contained all the flaws and foibles of mortals. So a free people must confine government. To him, good intentions plus political power equaled tyranny all too often.

If the world is no smarter today than it was when C. S. Lewis died in 1963, we certainly can't blame him. He gifted us wisdom by the bushels—wisdom we ignore at our peril.

## J. GRESHAM MACHEN

Of the Presbyterian theologian J. Gresham Machen (1881–1937), Pulitzer Prize-winning novelist and Nobel laureate Pearl S. Buck declared: "The man was admirable. He never gave in one inch to anyone. He never bowed his head. It was not in him to trim or compromise, to accept any peace that was less than triumph. He was a glorious enemy because he was completely open and direct in his angers and hatreds. He stood for something and everyone knew what it was."

Lest you be tempted to dismiss Buck's praise as biased—because, after all, she was raised by Presbyterian missionaries living in China—consider the view of H. L. Mencken.

Mencken was known for his caustic criticisms of Christians in general and ministers in particular. He described the Creator as "a comedian whose audience is afraid to laugh" and once wrote: "Shave a gorilla and it would be almost impossible, at twenty paces, to distinguish him from a heavyweight champion of the world. Skin a chimpanzee, and it would take an autopsy to prove he was not a theologian."

But Mencken pronounced great admiration for J. Gresham Machen:

Dr. Machen is surely no mere soap-boxer of God, alarming bucolic sinners for a percentage of the plate. On the contrary, he is a man of great learning.... His moral advantage over his Modernist adversaries, like his logical advantage, is immense and obvious. He faces the onslaught of the Higher Criticism without flinching, and he yields nothing of his faith to expediency or decorum.

When Machen died, Mencken compared him to another prominent Presbyterian, politician William Jennings Bryan, with these words: "Dr. Machen was to Bryan as the Matterhorn is to a wart."

Machen exhibited remarkable courage and logical consistency that I wish were more common within Christian leadership. His convictions were deep and thoroughly reasoned. He saw liberty as God's intention for humanity and would not abide the presumptuous claims of earthly governments to diminish it for our own good. The man was fearlessly principled.

Machen resolved to defend conservative Reformed theology against the growing influence of the modernists, the theological wing of the "progressive" movement that watered down traditional Christian beliefs and elevated such dubious notions as moral relativism and activist government. He proved a worthy antagonist to the religious left.

Machen was not a theological "fundamentalist"; he was too scholarly for that. He appreciated science as a tool for unraveling the mysteries of an ordered universe. His best-known books were systematic and thorough defenses of Christianity (for example, *The Origin of Paul's Religion* and *What Is Faith?*) and devastating critiques of modernist revisionism (such as *Christianity and Liberalism*) that remain influential nearly a century later.

Machen didn't much care for politics. He saw it as inherently stifling and anti-individual. He believed it was a dangerous fiction to portray true Christianity as to even a small degree compatible with any form of statism—socialism, communism, or fascism. Historian George Marsden, in his 1991 book *Understanding Fundamentalism and Evangelicalism*, labels Machen's political views as "radical libertarian" because the theologian "opposed almost any extension of state power." Machen might have been happy with the description, but he would have seen it as a natural extension of the teachings of Christ, who advocated character building and spiritual renewal and not state power.

Machen spoke out against U.S. involvement in World War I and condemned the Versailles Treaty as "an attack on international peace" that would produce war after war "in a wearisome progression." He deemed the overseas interventions of President Woodrow Wilson—a close family friend—as starry-eyed adventurism. He denounced conscription, arguing that the draft represented an assault on freedom and a "brutal interference" with the individual and with family life.

When a proposed child labor amendment to the Constitution grabbed headlines in the 1920s, Machen slammed it as "one of the most cruel and heartless measures that have ever been proposed in the name of philanthropy." He understood the economics of a measure outlawing any employment for children under the age of eighteen: it would either drive child labor underground and into deplorable conditions or would relegate poor families to even greater poverty. More important to Machen was what the amendment represented: a federal usurpation of a matter more properly left to the states, localities, and families.

At a time when the overwhelming majority of Presbyterians supported alcohol prohibition, Machen fought it. Scripture cautions against inebriation, he argued, but nowhere does it suggest government coercion as the solution.

He objected to Bible reading and prayer in public schools because they mixed politics with faith; Christians, he said, should form their own schools. He believed it was foolish to think that government would produce anything but a soul-crushing, collectivist mediocrity in the classroom:

> Place the lives of children in their formative years, despite the convictions of their parents, under the intimate control of experts appointed by the state, force them to attend schools where the higher aspirations of humanity are crushed out, and where the mind is filled with the materialism of the day, and it is difficult to see how even the remnants of liberty can subsist.

Machen was only fifty-five when he died, on New Year's Day 1937, after contracting pleurisy that developed into pneumonia. He never lived to see the rise of the Great Society, let alone the resurgent popularity of socialism in our day. But this New Testament scholar and devout Christian left little doubt how he would have responded to these trends. He made his views plain in his book *The Christian Faith in the Modern World* (1936), where he wrote:

> Everywhere there rises before our eyes the spectre of a society where security, if it is attained at all, will be attained at the expense of freedom, where the security that is attained will be the security of fed beasts in a stable, and where all the high aspirations of humanity will have been crushed by an all-powerful state.

## THE QUESTION AT HAND

C. S. Lewis and J. Gresham Machen were brilliant thinkers. Both sought faithfully to explain Scripture and its true meaning as best they could. They exerted great influence within Christianity and beyond. To the question "Was Jesus a socialist?" I believe both would answer, "Of course not."

Conclusion

# THE IRON FIST IN
# THE VELVET GLOVE

Socialism is an iron fist wrapped in a velvet glove. From the outside, it looks reasonable and appealing. *The state will care for you! The state will relieve you of many worries and responsibilities! The state will give you free stuff! The state will help the poor and punish the rich!*

Inside that velvet glove, however, you'll find force and compulsion. Socialism is about political and economic power; its promises to care for you are the bait.

Nearly two centuries ago, Frédéric Bastiat clearly explained socialism, both the sources of its appeal and its fatal flaws. Socialists declare, he said, that the state "should intervene directly to relieve all suffering, satisfy and anticipate all wants, furnish capital to all enterprises, enlightenment to all minds, balm for all wounds, [and] asylums for all the unfortunate."

As Bastiat recognized, this all *sounds* wonderful: "Who would not like to see all these benefits flow forth upon the world from the law, as from an inexhaustible source?"

Who indeed? Socialism's resurgent popularity in twenty-first-century America speaks to the appeal of this message.

But Bastiat followed with the essential caveat: "Certainly, we would like to have all this, *if it were possible.*" So is it possible?

No, it's not. Bastiat explained why. The state has nothing to give anybody except what it first takes from somebody. "Whence does [the state] draw those resources that it is urged to dispense by way of benefits to individuals? Is it not from the individuals themselves? How, then, can these resources be increased by passing through the hands of a parasitic and voracious intermediary?" All government will do is "absorb many useful resources," while robbing people of "a part of their freedom, along with a part of their well-being."

Bad people are everywhere, but nothing brings them forth and licenses them to do evil more than this: *concentrated power.* Add to that the subordination of morality to the service of the secular state and you have a prescription for destruction.

But the state is the entity that socialists and progressives seek to elevate and empower. Government is not some magical fairy that sprinkles happy dust on its subjects. It is composed of mortals, prone to the temptations all mortals face.

The nineteenth-century American social commentator William Graham Sumner commented on the temptations of power and what they have wrought: "All history is only one long story to this effect: men have struggled for power over their fellow-men in order that they might win the joys of earth at the expense of others and might shift the burdens of life from their own shoulders upon those of others."

Socialists and their progressive allies pursue power, ostensibly for the "common good." But power is often at odds with what Jesus preached: love. Love is about affection and respect; power is about control. Another nineteenth-century commentator, the British writer William Hazlitt, said it well: "The love of liberty is the love of others; the love of power is the love of ourselves."

As we have seen, Jesus was no friend of concentrated earthly power. He never made false or unaffordable promises. He didn't curry favor with certain constituencies at the expense of others. He didn't play cynical class-warfare games. He focused on eternal truths, not temporary, earthly advantages. Not once did he advocate the initiation of force, nor did he ever suggest that good intentions justified the initiation of force.

In Jesus's teachings and in many other parts of the New Testament, Christians—indeed, all people—are advised to be of generous spirit, to care for one's family, to help the poor, to assist widows and orphans, to exhibit kindness, and to maintain the highest character. You can translate all that into the dirty business of coercive, vote-buying, politically driven redistribution schemes only if you read the Bible without paying attention—or if you're willing to distort the teachings to advance a political agenda.

In the final analysis, Jesus would never endorse a scheme that doesn't work and is rooted in envy and theft. Despite the attempts of modern-day progressives to make him into a welfare-state redistributionist, Jesus was nothing of the sort.

Remember that the next time you hear someone say, "Jesus was a socialist." Now you know the truth. Pass it on.

# Acknowledgments

I wish to thank several friends for their influence on the thoughts that shaped this book.

Pastor Dan Dickerson of Calvary Baptist Church in Midland, Michigan, gave me a small book when I attended his church a quarter century ago. The book, by Josh McDowell, was titled *More Than a Carpenter.* Written for an intelligent skeptic, it settled in my mind forever that Jesus was indeed who he said he was. Another pastor of mine during the time I lived in Midland is Reverend David Sarafolean of Christ Covenant Church, whose excellent sermons reinforced my understanding of the Christian message.

Historian Burton Folsom of Atlanta, Georgia, offered helpful suggestions during the writing of my first draft, as did Senior Pastor David E. Kent of the Fellowship of Praise in Stafford, Texas.

Jed Donahue at the Intercollegiate Studies Institute granted permission to incorporate certain portions of my 2016 book, *Real Heroes: Inspiring True Stories of Courage,*

*Character, and Conviction*, into this book, particularly the sections pertaining to Augustine, Anne Frank, and J. Gresham Machen. Jed suggested many excellent improvements as we worked together from first draft to final copy. He's the best editor I know.

My friend from across the pond, Daniel Hannan, graciously supplied a superb foreword. I've admired his stalwart defense of freedom and sound economics as an elected member of the European Parliament (pre-Brexit, of course).

For nearly eleven years (2008–2019), I served as president of a venerable organization, the Foundation for Economic Education (FEE.org). My earliest readings in matters of liberty and free markets came in the form of publications from FEE. I retired into a very active president emeritus role in May 2019. My gratitude for the influence FEE has had on my life and for the wonderful work of its fantastic staff today is boundless. I urge every reader to visit the FEE website on a daily basis.

One of the reasons I've had the time to work on this book as FEE's president emeritus is the support of the Humphreys family of Joplin, Missouri. I carry another title at FEE, that of Humphreys Family Senior Fellow. I extend my deep appreciation to Ethelmae Humphreys (my "Missouri Mom"); her daughter, Sarah; and her son, David.

In 2015, FEE published a small pamphlet I wrote, *Rendering unto Caesar: Was Jesus a Socialist?* This book expands on the arguments I first laid out in that essay. In fact, I've incorporated most of that pamphlet verbatim within this book. Other parts of certain chapters here first appeared as articles FEE published.

Regrettably, I don't have room here to mention by name the many other friends who, often in small but meaningful ways, have influenced me and my thinking. They all share this in common: *character*. I've come to believe that next to getting your relationship to God and your spiritual life in order, there's nothing of greater earthly importance than that.

Those men and women I've known to put a premium on honesty, patience, humility, generosity, gratitude, responsibility, self-discipline, and courage are the kind this troubled world needs so many more of!

# About the Author

**Lawrence W. Reed** is president emeritus of the Foundation for Economic Education (FEE), where he also holds the positions of Humphreys Family Senior Fellow and Ron Manners Global Ambassador for Liberty. He served as president of FEE for nearly eleven years before he retired in May 2019. Prior to taking the helm at FEE, Reed served for twenty-one years as president of the Mackinac Center for Public Policy. He also taught economics full-time at Northwood University, where he chaired the department of economics.

Reed is the author or editor of several other books, including *Excuse Me, Professor: Challenging the Myths of Progressivism* and *Real Heroes: Inspiring True Stories of Courage, Character, and Conviction* (ISI Books). A frequent guest on radio and television, he has written thousands of articles, and he delivers dozens of speeches each year. His speaking has taken him to dozens of countries around the world.

Reed holds a BA in economics from Grove City College and an MA in history from Slippery Rock State University, both in Pennsylvania. He holds honorary doctorates from Central Michigan University and Northwood University.

A native of Pennsylvania and a thirty-year resident of Michigan, Reed now resides in Newnan, Georgia. Visit his website, LawrenceWReed.com.

# We Invite You to Advance Liberty With Us.

The Foundation for Economic Education is the premier source for understanding the humane values of a free society, and the economic, legal, & ethical principles that make it possible. At FEE, students and their mentors explore freedom's limitless possibilities through seminars, classroom resources, social media, daily content, and free online courses, **all available at FEE.org.**

# FEE

EST. 1946